REMI
DE ROO

To Mel,
with best regards!
+ Remi J. De Roo
March 19, 2013

REMI DE ROO

Chronicles of a Vatican II Bishop

Remi De Roo

Foreword by Jean-Claude Cardinal Turcotte

NOVALIS

© 2012 Novalis Publishing Inc.

Cover design: Rick Blechta
Layout: Audrey Wells

Interior photographs: All photographs are courtesy of the author, except where otherwise noted.

Published by Novalis

Publishing Office
10 Lower Spadina Avenue, Suite 400
Toronto, Ontario, Canada
M5V 2Z2

Head Office
4475 Frontenac Street
Montréal, Québec, Canada
H2H 2S2

www.novalis.ca

Library and Archives Canada Cataloguing in Publication

De Roo, Remi J.   Remi De Roo : chronicles of a Vatican II bishop / Remi De Roo.

Issued also in an electronic format. ISBN 978-2-89646-471-5

    1. De Roo, Remi J. 2. Catholic Church--British Columbia--Victoria--Bishops--Biography. 3. Bishops--British Columbia--Victoria--Biography. I. Title.

BX4705.D436A3 2012   282.092   C2012-903872-5

Printed in Canada.

We acknowledge the financial support of the Government of Canada through the Canada Book Fund for business development activities.

5   4   3   2   16   15   14   13   12

To all people of good will,
living or deceased,
who enriched my life
as a pilgrim of Vatican II

BOOKS BY REMI DE ROO

Man to Man (with Douglas Roche) – The Bruce Publishing Company, 1969

Cries of Victims, Voice of God – Novalis/Lorimer, 1986

À Cause de l'Évangile –Novalis, 1988

In the Eye of the Catholic Storm (with Mary Jo Leddy and Douglas Roche) – Harper Collins, 1992

Even Greater Things (with Mae and Bernard Daly) – Novalis, 1999

Biblical Characters and the Enneagram: Images of Transformation (with Diane Tolomeo and Pearl Gervais) – Newport Bay Publishing, 2001

ACKNOWLEDGEMENTS

Many hands, eyes and minds go into the making of a book, and I wish to acknowledge the encouragement, support and assistance of the people who helped this work emerge into the light of day.

First, I owe deep gratitude to His Eminence Jean-Claude Cardinal Turcotte, Archbishop Emeritus of Montreal, for honouring me with the Foreword to the book. His advice, wisdom and encouragement have sustained me through many years.

Sincere thanks go to Marisa Antonini, who urged me to write this story and provided generous initial funding for the project.

I am grateful to Joe Sinasac, publishing director of Novalis, and my editor, Anne Louise Mahoney. Novalis's belief in the value of this project and their willingness to undertake it encouraged me immensely. Working with them was a pleasure.

The birthing of these chronicles would never have occurred had it not been for my many friends who provided support, confidence, encouragement, assistance and even some prodding. The three members of the Project Team behind this book deserve special credit. All three put their hearts and energy into this venture. They saw its scope, potential and importance. The Honourable Douglas Roche, O.C., has proven to be like a brother to me. He overcame my reticence, empowered me and volunteered to be my agent. I was the beneficiary of his experience, generosity and determination. Diane Tolomeo used her literary acumen and creative skills to coordinate my reflections, feelings and experiences, collate my random thoughts into a coherent product, and enhance my prose. Pearl Gervais helped me to awaken my memory, assisted in research and the assembling of all the material for these chronicles, sustained my energy and enthusiasm, and watched over my health as the project unfolded.

I thank Chris and Tom Loughlin, Pat Clark and Suzanne Heymann for providing me with editorial assistance in many and varied forms. Very special thanks go to Patrick Jamieson and Ray Painchaud for helping me gather the photos used in the book. Patrick Deroover, Lynn Haley, Linda Jonk, Joe Milner, Paul Paniccia, Larry Samuels and Olivia Varin-Bernier also assisted me in recovering photos taken over many decades.

Among my consultants in various matters – pastoral, historic, literary, theological and legal – were Patricia Brady, osb, Chris Considine Q.C., Kevin Doyle, David Gurr, Monsignor Michael Lapierre, and Anthony Sebastian, ofm.

I also express my thanks for their contributions to my other friends and colleagues: the IHM Sisters of Tofino, the Benedictine Sisters of Nanaimo, the Poor Clares Sisters of Duncan, Fr. Pat Clark, Tony Clarke, Dani Dooher, Peter Gubbels, Robert Kaiser, Vicki Marston, Maureen Ranaghan and Jack Sproule, as well as some other donors who requested anonymity.

I wish to acknowledge my family (locally and internationally), as well as associates and neighbours for their interest and loving support through the entire span of this project.

+ Remi De Roo
March 31, 2012

CONTENTS

FOREWORD

Bishop Remi De Roo is a man of passion and commitment. As I read the pages of his life and work in preparation for writing this foreword, which he graciously invited me to do, those initial characteristics were confirmed. The title of the book could not have been better chosen. Bishop De Roo was and remains a bishop of Vatican II.

Periodically, it happens that I hear priests or young Christians speak of the Council as if it were of a very early era. I hear it spoken of as a significant piece of ancient history. Its documents could be catalogued in archives set alongside those of the Council of Trent. However, what a great Council Vatican II was! It is still far from having produced all its fruits.

I was ordained a priest in May of 1959. On the 25th of January that year, Pope John XXIII advised the cardinals of his intention to call an ecumenical council. Thus my life as a priest began at the time when the Vatican Council was launched. I was then a Catholic Action chaplain in Montreal. Subsequently, while studying Social Sciences at the University of Lille, I followed the progress of the Council with avid interest. I am very conscious how deeply Vatican II impacted my apostolic life. Not only did it change my understanding of my role as a priest, but it also greatly influenced my life as the bishop I became.

In 1982, I joined the college of Canadian Bishops. It was evident that most of them had been fashioned by the Council experience. Such was the case with Bishop De Roo. The Bishop of Victoria at that time is the same one I see today. In reading the manuscript he sent me, which basically tells of his life as a bishop, I discovered even more clearly how the Vatican II documents structured his thinking and inspired his actions. His involvement with the Native peoples, his promotion of ecumenism, his concern that more importance be given to lay people within the faith communities, and especially his desire to see the Church present to and in the world in order to have the Gospel message of Jesus Christ better known and lived – all of that impressed me about him.

He and I have not always been in full agreement on everything. Still, we were always able to discuss issues, inspired by an authentic search for truth and a firm attachment to the Church.

Bishop De Roo invited me to preface his memoirs in the year in which we celebrate the 50th anniversary of the calling of the Second Vatican Council as well as the 50th anniversary of his episcopate. This story enlightens us as to the essential aims and dynamics of Vatican II. It helps us understand what the Church really is. Far from being a monolithic structure that grants only some of its members the right to voice and speech, the Church is a hospitable home where freedom to reflect, to believe and to express oneself is encouraged and validated. Isn't this one of the beautiful fruits of the Council's Declaration on Religious Freedom (*Dignitatis Humanae*)?

As you read the pages that follow, you will discover how Bishop De Roo applied the orientations of Vatican II to his diocese. His convictions were firm. He never compromised them, despite the criticisms and painful moments he endured. Now, retired, he relentlessly "preaches the story of Vatican II," so convinced is he that to preach it is to proclaim the Gospel for today. He does this while still confident that the Council inaugurated a process of conversion and renewal that concerns and calls forth the entire Church and each one of its members.

I sincerely hope that his book will be read by many people, regardless of their beliefs.

Jean-Claude Cardinal Turcotte
Archbishop Emeritus of Montreal
February 8, 2012

INTRODUCTION

"Remi, when are you going to write your life story?" For years, friends and acquaintances had been urging me to write this book. The badgering persisted, to the point that I started to ask them why. They gave me several reasons: my unique experience in life, as the "boy bishop" who had participated in all four Vatican Council II sessions; the remarkable contrast between myself as a farm boy from the rolling terrain of Manitoba to my life as a bishop on an island in the Pacific; and my sometimes controversial work as head of the Diocese of Victoria, Canada.

People were concerned about how to share their faith more effectively with their children and neighbours. They wanted to hear of what had sustained me these many years and motivated me to do all I did. They asked questions about the relationship between faith and justice, whether the Church is still relevant, and if I could somehow give them the hope they so desperately sought. Despite theirs urgings, I kept finding reasons to decline, until they finally convinced me that my life has been so rich in meaningful experiences that I had a duty to share it. After prayer and reflection, I came to realize that although this story is my personal memoir, it is enriched by the energy and inspiration of many people who have helped me become who I am. Indeed, each of our stories is a God-story, full of moments like the one in which the Gospel of Luke depicts Mary proclaiming that "the Almighty has done great things for me."

As I began to write, I felt keenly a renewed awakening and a surging of my farm roots. The image of the farm and its garden became a metaphor for my own life. I remain at heart a farm boy who, like Abraham with Sarah, was called to leave his land and his family to enter into a new land that God would show him. Ordained to the ministerial priesthood, I accepted a call and a mission that has led me to wider horizons.

In 1962, to my surprise, I was appointed to the Episcopate at age 38. Despite my apprehensions about the future, in my inner heart I was confident and at peace as I knelt before the three ordaining bishops on December 14. I have always believed that with the divine call come the graces required for the mission and the courage to face its challenges. I resolved to do my utmost to follow in the footsteps of Christ, the servant leader. I chose as my motto "Building in Love" (Eph. 4.16).

In retrospect, my ordination could not have happened at a more propitious time. Coming during the first session of the Second Vatican Council, it allowed me to orient my leadership as Bishop of Victoria according to the vision of the saintly Pope John XXIII and to the aspirations contained in the documents of Vatican II. With my people, we would consider the signs of the times, the call to renewal, and the return to our origins, developing appropriate ways to respond to the presence of the Spirit in modern times. One of Pope John's legacies was to add the dimension of friendship to the central insight of communion that is now common in our somewhat antiquated Church vocabulary. In his broad chest beat a heart that embraced all of humankind, unconditionally. More than anyone else, he transformed the dominant symbol of the Vatican II from that of a pyramid, with vertical lines of authority, seeking to impart wisdom unilaterally, to that of a circle, with all members equal in dignity and in capacity to serve. Every disciple listens and is taught. This was the dream for which I have devoted my life. That is what my memoir is about.

"A farmer went out to sow his seed," says the Gospel of Matthew (13.3). My diocese became the new land to which God had led me. With the guidance of the Spirit, I attempted as best I could to nurture the people, to cultivate, to fertilize, to live through the storms that might have devastating effects. Farmers live in hope, in anticipation. They depend on propitious circumstances beyond themselves. Their life is a collaboration with the Creator. So, too, was my life. Together with the people in the diocese, our harvesting time came to further fruition, a process culminating in the celebration of our Diocesan Assembly in 1986, *Forward in the Spirit*.

My happiest moment as a bishop occurred at the conclusion in 1991 of the five-year People's Synod held throughout Vancouver Island. More than a thousand people gathered at the grassroots level of parishes and groups to discern where they were going as Church in our society and our modern culture. Were there new ways to evangelize? Were there new signs of the times to address? What is the Gospel saying to us here and now, and which we may perhaps have to learn to reconsider anew? How do we as Christians continue to be people of hope and joy? As a farmer, I was conscious that one must always be attentive to adapting. Much of the machinery and tools used when I was a boy are unrecognizable now. This gave me a sense of moving forward but benefiting from the wisdom of our elders.

When I invited the members of our diocese to enter into the synod process, I was delighted with the response. It was as if a fresh spring rain had come to nourish them. They gathered in groups with respect and wisdom, listening, feeling and responding. People shared and prayed over their hopes and dreams, griefs and sorrows. These sessions were the fodder from which working papers and proposals emerged. Those proposals were offered to the 90 synod delegates at the formal sessions. There, the delegates, chosen by the parishes, learned to voice their visions, to deepen their spirituality of living faith and to discern modern ways of living it more fully.

This was no small challenge! I watched, listened and marvelled at how the assembly addressed everyday realities from sexuality to spirituality, family to community, justice to peace. Gradually, we perceived that the dominant symbol of our faith family was moving from the vertical lines of the pyramid, with communications coming down from the top, to the more inclusive circle, where all are equals even when their responsibilities vary.

The synod proved to be a highlight in my many years of episcopal ministry. I was greatly elated and felt truly blessed to have been able to see this process unfold. It brought to life much of the energy I had felt diffused throughout the Vatican Council. It illustrated clearly to me how the Holy Spirit is present to people of faith when they take a step forward in their pursuit of the Reign of God. As we gathered in circles on that final day, I knew instinctively that my life as a priest and bishop had matured. I would probably never have a happier moment.

After my retirement at age 75, I decided to "re-tire," to put on "new tires," to accept further invitations to lecture and to visit new lands. Travels, lectures and workshops in Canada, the United States, Europe and China have enriched this farm boy immensely. Matthew, at the end of his gospel, speaks of Jesus inviting his followers to go to all nations. In this memoir, I attempt to describe the thoughts, feelings and actions of such privileged work with so many, with "all my relations," as my Aboriginal friends are wont to say. I have found that every land is one flowing with milk and honey; every land is holy. They are all diverse in nature but full of beauty, wisdom and possibilities, just as I knew on the farm that some crops are more successful on certain types of soil; that each crop in some way feeds and sustains God's creatures, be they the birds that fly, the flowers that bloom in the fields, or human beings, spirits enfleshed, created in God's image.

One modest book cannot possibly do justice to an enterprise as vast, rich and complex as Vatican II. Numerous books will continue to be published, sharing an endless variety of interpretations. Vatican II succeeded in obtaining an extraordinary consensus of leaders coming from a variety of schools of thought. I personally experienced the uplifting and inspiring atmosphere present in St. Peter's. I know that what all the bishops, without exception, wanted to achieve was to give our Church a renewed impulse whereby it could more lovingly and effectively present gospel values that Jesus brought into a world hungering for truth, justice with compassion, and lasting peace. Post–Vatican II publications seem to deal primarily with arguments pro and con certain intellectual perceptions. But as a pastoral Council, Vatican II enhanced our understanding of the Gospel message as we seek to apply it to our daily life. Its pastoral side encompasses more than doctrines, essential as they are. My intent here has more to do with vision and motivation than with theological dissertations, fascinating as they may be. The followers of Jesus Christ are pilgrims engaged in a way of life faithful to the truth revealed definitively by the Son of God, made visible, tangible, dwelling in our hearts, walking with us towards God's Reign.

In the pages that follow, I share with you some of the experiences that have enriched my life. This chronicle contains events and experiences well beyond the Diocese of Victoria. Where the next part of my life will lead is in God's hands. But since I am a part of all that I have met, that includes all of you, my readers, my friends. I invite you to peruse these pages and take delight not only in my life, but in yours as well.

PART ONE

FROM FARM BOY
TO COUNCIL FATHER

LIFE ON THE FARM

"Your mother is dead. Now don't cry." My grandmother used these words to inform me of my mother's death when I arrived home from St. Boniface College after being summoned. The stoic part of me rose to the challenge and I held back my tears. Moments later we all walked to the nearby church. The pastor had thoughtfully delayed the funeral until the afternoon arrival of the train so I could be there. Kneeling close to Mother's open casket, I caught my last glimpse of the cherished woman who had gifted me with life. I was fifteen years old; she was only 47. The year was 1939.

She and my older sister, Gerarda, had just come to visit me for my birthday (on February 24) during my first year at the college. It was bitterly cold. The 100-mile train ride back to Swan Lake, Manitoba, was long and arduous. Mother contracted pneumonia doubled with pleurisy and died within four days. The antibiotics that might have saved her life were as yet unavailable.

I knew nothing of this. My cousin Clara De Pape, who worked as a nurse in St. Boniface, came to the college to accompany me home. She told me that my mother was desperately ill and I had been called home, but said nothing more than that. When we got to Swan Lake,

Clara and I went to our grandparents' home, which was close to both the station and the church. Upon our arrival, my grandmother met me at the door with those words I will never forget. It was a terrible shock.

Josephine Elodie De Pape remains etched in my memory as a beautiful and delicate woman with a wry sense of humour. She was the life of the small parties held on rare occasions in our home. She was also highly sensitive and easily hurt. One day, returning from church in our car, she was weeping. Gossiping neighbours had launched some barbs in her direction and she responded with tears. I will never forget my father gently trying to console her, to calm her down, and to persuade her that she should ignore such gossip.

I have fond memories of myself as a little boy accompanying her to the garden that she tended with such great devotion and practical knowledge. Together we would dig up some of the big weeds. She would invite me to drape them over the fence to dry out. Then she would encourage me to invent imaginary stories of where these weeds came from and what stories they might have to tell us. But she was also sickly, with a touch of sadness about her. She had difficulty relaxing.

After her death, I watched my father, who never remarried, struggle with the stresses of heading a single-parent family of eight. It was a difficult time for him. But I think that because of this (and, no doubt, other reasons), I have always found it easy to relate to people who are living in non-traditional family structures.

My father, Raymond Peter De Roo, was a serene and very likeable person. A man of few words, he was trusted by everyone, for it was well known that his word was gold. In business matters, his handshake would dispense with any paperwork. Contracts were not necessary when dealing with him. At home he was very attentive to his large family of five girls and three boys. He also had a lovely singing voice – a tenor – and was occasionally heard singing to himself. (His favorite melodies were "Ramona" and "Springtime in the Rockies.") It surprised no one that he was the leader of our small parish choir. He knew all the Gregorian masses by heart and would volunteer to sing one at the drop of a hat.

Father raised purebred registered shorthorn cattle, and we took some of our best animals to show. My father taught me how to groom them to look better than they actually were. White bull calves were less desirable as sires, but one time my father risked keeping one rather than sending it to market. He took it to the Brandon Fair and returned home radiant: not only had it won a championship, but he had managed to sell it to a Protestant! Thirty years later, when I was giving a lecture at the Peace Gardens near Deloraine, Manitoba, I found myself billeted with a Mr. Peter Dyck; it turned out his father had been the one who had bought that bull! I smile to think of this chain of events, and my amusement at it, as a pre-ecumenical story. At a time when interchurch relations were officially frowned upon, I remember my father being on friendly terms with every Protestant in our neighbourhood.

I never heard my father speak in anger or swear. He did not allow us to do other than absolutely necessary work on Sundays. The family recited the Rosary together daily, and of course we fasted before Mass. Had our grandparents not fed us afterwards, we would have ended up fasting until mid-afternoon.

All eight of us were born on the farm. I was a big baby, arriving on a Sunday morning at 10 a.m. "Just in time to say Mass," Father Everard Kwakman, the Flemish-speaking priest and family friend for whom my mother had been a housekeeper for a number of years before her marriage, later remarked. My father's brother Remi had died of influenza; calling me after him helped keep his memory alive.

My early childhood was marred by a succession of illnesses. I was told this but never knew the details. They did leave me with a frail physique; I envied my brother Michael, who soon surpassed me in height, weight and strength. I marvelled how even in sub-zero temperatures, he never wore mittens.

School was easy for me. St. Gerard's was only five minutes away, a one-room schoolhouse that went up to Grade 8, which most farm folk at the time considered enough education for their children. With all eight grades in one classroom, and a single teacher, the older children were expected to, and did, help the younger ones. I still take pride in the number of graduates of our little school who became leaders in society. My father, knowing the value of something he never had had himself, provided for all of us to get either a university education or a professional one.

The hired help were mostly seasonal workers for harvest time, with the exception of Rene Poppe, a distant relative of my father's, who lived with us all year round. The others slept on hay in the barn, which offered a modicum of comfort. At threshing time we worked under heavy pressures in a rather rough-and-tumble atmosphere. With a somewhat delicate physique, I endured more than my share of verbal and even, on occasion, physical abuse.

All the workers needed to be fed five times a day. We were up at 5 a.m. for chores, then had our breakfast at 6:00 a.m. At 9 a.m., those hauling grain were charged with bringing lunch to the fields: buns, sandwiches, cakes and copious quantities of tea and coffee. At noon we fed the horses, then ourselves, and were back to work at 1 p.m. At 3:30 p.m. it was time for more food; supper was at sundown. After our last chores, we went to bed around 10 p.m. On reflection, I am amazed at the dedicated labour of the women of that era. They got even less sleep than the men and had to observe the regular routine of cleaning and laundry over and above the massive amounts of food prepared and served on schedule – all without electricity or the labour-saving devices taken for granted today.

There were some basic rules we learned that served us all our lives. One was that work came first and had to be finished before we would be allowed playtime. But while there was always a lot to be done on the farm, life was not all labour. I recall some of the games we used to play. My sisters generally preferred games like hopscotch or skipping rope. They would also participate in team games such as "peggy" – which involved catapulting sticks, or "pegs" – and "anti-over," played with a soft ball thrown over a low building to be caught by the opposing side, who then sought to tag one of the opponents.

Boys' games centred on playing baseball, trapping gophers and, later on, shooting them with a .22 calibre rifle. In the autumn, hunting took over: whitetail deer and ducks, geese, grouse and partridges, and we set wire snares for rabbits. My father once told me that in their first years in Canada they regularly caught many bush rabbits, which provided a welcome source of fresh meat.

I have many other recollections from my childhood – some happy and some sad. I remember frequent sleigh rides through snowdrifts in the winter, whether for work or recreation; herding cattle along the road allowances during the Depression, looking for patches of green grass to supplement what was no longer available in dried-out pastures; and, as a seven-year-old, walking barefoot before attending school, and running about after a rain, feeling the mud squishing between my toes. When not in school, we were sent to tend the cows as they grazed: we had to make sure they did not break through the fences that surrounded the crops. This was not only to save the grain but also to protect the cows: eating fresh green alfalfa could cause them to become severely bloated, and could even kill them. I once stared in awe, heart pounding, as my father plunged a knife into a bloated cow's belly to relieve the pressure, hoping to save its life. And I once felt very mournful as I watched a hired hand dig a large pit in which to bury a favourite horse that had died from sleeping sickness.

Once, when I was about eleven years old, I was standing in a runaway wagon, holding some newly purchased dishes that I had been instructed to bring back from town. Two cousins had dared each other to race their empty wagons back to the threshing site. One had dropped a rein and was pulling on the other to slow the horses, but only succeeding in forcing them to veer wildly into a deep ditch. The wagon rolled over with me inside, luckily without serious injury. Not a single dish was broken.

I have much earlier memories of catching my middle finger in a gopher trap. Lacking the strength to open the spring-loaded device, I had no choice but to walk home dragging the trap behind me. I recall homework done during winter evenings with a gas pressure lamp, and kerosene lanterns in the barns for late-night chores. At age twelve I pleaded with my parents for my own corner of the garden where I could experiment with growing new varieties of vegetables, and was granted the privilege. The result was that I won first prize for a bunch of "coreless" carrots. I also managed to grow a new variety of sweet red rhubarb. We filled the back seat and trunk of our car with large specimens of vegetable marrow, then drove to town to pack its contents into a railway car of relief food for starving people in the province of Saskatchewan during the great drought of the dirty thirties.

Sensing my interest in the priesthood, our local parish priest, Monsignor Boniface Deiderichs, recommended to my parents that they enroll me, after Grade 8, in the Jesuit-run College in Saint Boniface. This was an exclusively French institution promoting the liberal arts. My first language was Flemish, and I had learned English at around age seven. Now here I was, 14, faced with the enormous challenge of being initiated into another completely new language under a stern regime and considerable academic pressure. Arriving at my new residence in September, with exclusively francophone fellow students, I scrambled to learn the language. At Christmas I found myself facing the dilemma of either writing my exams in French or not writing them at all. I wrote them as required. (By my third year, when reading my English algebra manual, I found myself thinking in French. This experience encouraged me to learn several languages over the years.)

During my first Christmas home, my father, as head of the choir, thought that since I now spoke French, I should take over the task of singing the customary "Minuit Chrétiens" to open the liturgy on the dot of midnight. Thus I found myself up in the choir loft, assigned to sing a solo in my newly acquired language on a moment's notice. And so I did.

I was a sickly child for most of my youth and seemed to catch every illness that came my way. When a wave of measles hit most of the students, I came down with scarlet fever and spent a month in isolation in the hospital. A young nursing sister from the Grey Nuns community looked after me. Years later she confided to me that she was almost distraught at the possibility of losing her very first patient. All I remember of that time is the sound emanating from her starched linen frock and the clicking of rosary beads as she approached my bed. These sounds were comforting to me, for they meant that someone nearby was watching and that I had avoided the deafness that often follows this illness.

The Grey Nuns offered free room and board to four students who were willing to serve early morning Mass and occasional special liturgical events at the hospital. Given my limited financial resources, I promptly signed up. To help defray the costs of my tuition, I also tended a small corner shop that sold a variety of refreshments and sweets, sharpened hockey skates, mended broken hockey sticks, and helped convert the college playing fields into ice rinks. This meant tending a water hose through the long night hours, sprinkling the frozen ground attentively, layer by layer, until successive coats of ice developed into a solid skating surface. Snow removal was the responsibility of the players themselves.

I never became a good skater, but my reflexes were excellent and I had good peripheral vision. Hence, I was soon designated as a goalkeeper for the hockey team, and rapidly rose in rank to play for one of the more advanced teams. After a memorable season, in the final game, with the championship at stake, our team was leading by one goal. A formidable opponent got a breakaway and was bearing down on my net. Eyes on the puck, I promised myself he would not score. I woke up in the infirmary only to discover that I had made the save, but the puck had knocked me out. (This was a time long before goalies wore helmets, and I was not wearing one.) That accident brought our team victory, but it also ended my enchantment with the game.

I received my B.A. in Latin Philosophy in 1946 from the Collège de Saint-Boniface (University of Manitoba). I then registered for the Major Seminary to study for the ministerial priesthood.

As I reflect back on my schooling, I am aware of and grateful for its significant influence on my intellectual development. Occasionally I get the impression that people perceive me as being somewhat aloof, possibly even indifferent to their moods or emotional situations. Nothing could be further from the truth, but I learned to protect myself from strong emotions early in life: not to deny them, but to keep them well hidden. As I get older, I find it a bit easier to let these emotions out of their hiding places every now and then, and to befriend them when I do.

I began this part of my story with an account of the trauma I felt at my mother's death in 1939. My father died peacefully in July of 1975, but another emotional shock lay in store for me in 1977, with the sudden accidental death of my brother Michael, age 51, along with his son, Raymond, who was only 16. The two of them were overcome by methane fumes emanating from a liquid manure pit that was attached to the cow barn on the family farm. The shock to our family was enormous. As I was participating in the prayer vigil before the funeral, kneeling by their two coffins, a well-meaning friend gently tapped me on the shoulder and whispered in my ear, "It's all right to cry now." Instantly I froze. I continued to remain there, head bowed, eyes closed, in stunned silence. Having been given permission to cry now, and having been denied that choice so many years earlier when my mother died, I was unable and unwilling to cry on demand. I have since understood more clearly how these two shocks profoundly affected me. These two events, and my reactions to each of them, may help to explain my sometimes stoic appearance under pressure, when I do not feel free to simply emote, as well as my difficulty at times in sharing profound emotions. However, I truly believe that these experiences also made me very sensitive to other bereaved people, especially in tragic or unexpected situations.

Called to Serve

I do not recall any single dramatic moment in which I knew God was calling me to be a priest. My vocation developed quietly. There had always been an atmosphere of piety in our home, and a great respect for the priesthood. I looked forward to serving at Mass with other altar boys, when I was big enough to carry the Missal from one side of the altar to the other, genuflecting on the way without tripping. It was at college that I began to contemplate being ordained as a diocesan priest. The sense of service to people, combined with advanced studies and rewarding ministry, appealed to me. My pastor (affectionately still called "Father" Boniface even though he was by then a Monsignor) was certainly one of the chief influences in my early life. He was a highly educated man, widely read and wise. I believe that it was from his example that I initially caught the dream of becoming a priest.

My spirituality reflected the common understanding of the time, carrying a sense of fear of damnation if one was caught in mortal sin. Hell was frequently alluded to as what happened without fail to "bad" people. Regular confession was taken for granted as required for salvation. Popular devotions were considered the ideal way to grow in sanctity. The Rosary, a simple repetitive practice, was considered a standard and reliable way to pray. Like most other people, I would never have aspired to be a "mystic," unworthy as I considered myself of real spiritual greatness. That was left to the "real" saints whose lives we were encouraged to read about and emulate, and to admire them while avoiding all thoughts of our own holiness inspired by personal pride. Salvation was somewhat a bargaining process: if I behaved myself and fulfilled certain basic requirements, like going to church regularly, God in turn would receive me into heaven at the end of my days. Like many others, I did not miss a chance to gain indulgences.

My ordination to the ministerial priesthood will be forever etched in my memory.

Ordinations were always celebrated at the Cathedral, on Sundays. I desired very much to be ordained in my home parish of St. Martin of Tours, but knew the Archbishop could not be drawn away from the Cathedral on a Sunday. I eventually persuaded him to come instead to my home parish of Swan Lake on a Thursday, on the Feast of Corpus Christi, one of my favourites. Thus I was ordained on June 8, 1950. I celebrate annually on the feast of the Holy Eucharist, ignoring the calendar date.

I had a deep and warm feeling in my heart as I knelt before the ordaining Prelate. It seemed to me that the whole of my life could now be centred on the key mystery of our faith: God in the person of Jesus Christ becoming for all humankind the unending source of life, love and truth. In retrospect, however, I recognize how limited my theological horizons were at the time. I saw myself called primarily to provide leadership to a parish, as an educated person prepared to look after people and provide them with answers to their spiritual needs. I was still far removed from the future vision of Vatican II. I had not yet developed the sense of a global mission or of the relationships of my local community with other faith communities, the Church as a communion of communions and the local church as linked to the Church universal by bonds of charity. It remained for the Council to teach me to recognize that all baptized believers together constitute the people of God.

My Archbishop, Georges Cabana, was anxious to train effective teachers for his newly established seminary, and sought to find them in his own diocese. Even before my ordination at age 26, he had asked me to prepare for studies in Rome, with a view to obtaining a doctorate in theology. Italy opened up a whole new world to me, a farm boy finding himself in a land of great culture, and in a cosmopolitan city with sights and tastes unimagined in rural Manitoba. The popular expression "all roads lead to Rome" now conveyed a much deeper meaning. There I met fellow students from many countries. I enjoyed the vicinity of and access to St. Peter's Basilica, the Vatican and countless ancient monuments. In those two years, I came to appreciate how one can have a different global and even spiritual perspective when one is steeped in history, sensing more immediately the heartbeat of Catholicism and the cultural variety of its expressions.

I attended Dominican Angelicum University and boarded at the Canadian College with some 25 other priests. One of my professors, Father Gerard Geenen, of Flemish Belgian origin, agreed to be the moderator for my thesis. I felt truly privileged to be one of the few students whose thesis project he accepted to oversee and moderate each year. He proved to be a merciless taskmaster but a highly skilled advisor. Under his guidance I learned to appreciate the value of disciplined and patient research. Once he was satisfied with my work, he became a staunch supporter during the rigorous defense of my thesis. Under his tutelage, I completed my doctoral studies in two years instead of the usual three.

Life in a Parish

I enjoyed Rome but was glad to return to my roots when I was assigned as an associate pastor to the parish of Holy Cross in Norwood, Manitoba. Holy Cross was a very busy place. There were 1100 parishioners on our register, "mixed" marriages (as they were then called), and also many converts, who were generally among the most active participants. The parish rated at least one, and sometimes even two, assistant priests. We had two secretaries as well as a housekeeper. It was the only English-speaking parish in Saint Boniface. I soon made wonderful friends who both supported and challenged me in many ways.

The pastor, Father Charles Empson (later a Monsignor), and I soon became good friends. We agreed on a sharing of schedules, which included the understanding that I would gather his several prospective "converts" into one group and teach them as a class. In turn, he would give me a block of free time each afternoon so I could put the finishing touches on my doctoral thesis to refine and prepare it for publication. A distinguished French magazine, aptly named *Marie*, had offered to publish it in its entirety in a special issue. Given my limited financial means, I was very happy to be able to have my thesis published at no cost to me, for publication was a prerequisite for obtaining my degree.

My contact in the "convert class" with a growing number of non-Catholics opened my eyes, and my heart as well, to the possibility of greater outreach to people other than our own parishioners. I started an "Inquiry Forum," and access was open to all interested people, and there were no expectations placed on those who attended. All those who attended grew in their appreciation of the meaning of Christianity. And as with so many things, in instructing others, I, too, had my eyes opened in many ways to the workings of the Holy Spirit in people's hearts.

Such was the case with a woman I will call Mary Beth. Mary Beth came to me one day with a deep concern that was troubling her heart. She had married a Catholic man in a civil service, which meant he was no longer in regular communion with his church. She continued attending her own Protestant church, but her husband had completely ceased attending because of his civil marriage. She confided to me that he was quite unhappy, and she wanted me to have a talk with him. I met with the man, and I learned that he regretted his impulsive gesture, which had brought about his alienation, but did not know what to do about it. I invited him, along with their two teenaged daughters, to attend the Inquiry Forum, as a refresher course for him and as instruction in Catholicism for them. At the end of the sessions, he and his daughters told me that the girls wanted to be received into the Church, and he wanted to be welcomed back into it.

The Paschal celebration of the Easter Vigil arrived – the time when he would celebrate the sacrament of Reconciliation and the two girls would be baptized. I remember coming into the parish office next door to the church, and I noticed Mary Beth standing with her back to the wall and wearing a sad look on her face. I told her I felt it must be hard for her, in some sense, to see her husband and daughters moving into this new condition without her. She nodded and I could see the tears welling up in her eyes. Something inside of me led me to take the initiative and ask her if she would like to join them. She nodded in agreement. We had her inscribed among the candidates, then and there. I omitted the normally prescribed formalities, because I could see clearly that this was the work of the Holy Spirit, who had guided a non-Catholic person to bring her entire family into the Catholic Church.

An especially meaningful phase in my life was the time I spent as secretary to the Archbishop. Here I was initiated into the complex and sometimes very delicate matters that bishops are called to deal with. Archbishop Maurice Baudoux was a hard worker as well as a man with a global vision and a heart as big as the world. Year by year, he assigned a variety of new responsibilities to me. These constant changes created a situation in which my fellow priests began to ask, "Why can't Remi hold a job?"

I was initiated into another new sphere of life when I was appointed Secretary to the Manitoba Bishops' Conference, where I learned about politics as "the art of the possible" and the attitude of "politics as ideology." Prejudice and nose counting often won out over convictions around substantial issues. I was soon to learn the difference between statesmanship and partisan politics. I got some of my early introductions into the relationships between the Church and society. Several men from the parish became directly involved in the local political process, particularly with regard to the election of school trustees. I learned a lot about organization, strategies and the ways to get local people to accept civic responsibility.

I also taught medical ethics to the nurses in training at the St. Boniface Hospital. That experience afforded me priceless opportunities to apply to specific issues the principles of moral theology that I had been taught at college and seminary. I learned that there are many grey areas in life that fall between the black-and-white fields of theory, and that we are endowed with hearts and bodies as well as minds, all of which have a part in our decision making.

Over the years, while maintaining responsibilities from various assignments, I kept a connection with Holy Cross parish through weekend ministry. I loved this ongoing direct contact with pastoral life in its more visible and tangible forms. This experience also served me well when I was named pastor of the parish in 1960.

It was while I was presiding at an early weekday morning Mass that the news of my appointment as Bishop of Victoria was announced.

2

Plunged into the Renewal of the Church

There is something called the "Pontifical Secret," an agreement that certain information will not be revealed until the Pope has announced it. In October of 1962, I had already known for a week that I had been appointed Bishop of Victoria before it became public knowledge, but was bound by the Pontifical Secret to tell no one. It is not easy to continue with one's daily tasks and contacts while knowing that your life is about to change radically, and not being able to tell a single soul about it!

I received the word by way of a telephone call from Ottawa on October 23. A friend of mine, Father Lionel Bouvier, had teased me on occasion about my becoming a bishop, and I assumed this call was another one of his tricks. It dawned on me fairly quickly that this was the real thing: I was summoned to be in Ottawa the very next day, and no one was to know. This proved a bit tricky since I had my usual commitments in the parish. I contrived the ploy of saying casually to people that it seemed like good duck hunting weather, hoping they would assume my sudden disappearance was a spur of the moment duck-hunting expedition.

I left early the next morning. When the plane landed on a rainy tarmac in Ottawa, there was a flock of ducks in a puddle beside the airstrip! If anyone asked, I would be able to say I had indeed seen a lot of ducks. I had an audience with Monsignor Tagliaferri at 11 a.m. It finished 40 minutes later, and I was given 20 minutes until lunch at noon to go into the chapel and pray before rendering my decision. I accepted, and flew back to Manitoba the same day. As it was a "Bingo Boys" night, I went directly from the airport to the parish school hall to help clean up afterwards, sweeping up and holding the Pontifical Secret inside as I did the usual chores.

The parish had planned a series on Vatican II, which had been convened earlier that fall, and I was already scheduled to preach the next Sunday's sermon on the Council. It was a wonderful synchronicity that my topic, decided well before my trip to Ottawa, was on the role of the bishop. Our Archbishop was already in Rome at the Council; I had to preach without saying anything about my new status. After the sermon, I checked with the parish secretary to see if she had noticed anything different. She had not, and I was satisfied I could keep things quiet.

On October 30 I received an official letter that began "*Gaudio ex toto corde*" ("I rejoice with all my heart"), announcing my appointment as Bishop of the Diocese of Victoria. The next day – Halloween – the news was made public. Whether it was a trick or a treat, I was relieved of the Pontifical Secret. And on November 6, I was called to Rome, since all residential bishops were required to attend the Second Vatican Council. In the Latin tradition, the candidate appointed as a bishop immediately has jurisdiction over the territory to which he is assigned. I was to assume this responsibility even before my episcopal ordination.

I will never forget how awestruck I was walking into St. Peter's Basilica for the first time as a new bishop. My first experience of Vatican II lingers in my memory like a wonderful dream. With my youthful impressions that a bishop was the equivalent of a prince, I was literally overwhelmed by the Catholic Episcopate in its entirety, assembled in Saint Peter's in Rome. In their episcopal regalia, with the brilliant lighting flooding the immense Basilica, they looked like a gathering of the saints in the antechamber to heaven.

It took time for me to accustom myself to all this grandeur, pomp and circumstance. But the reality of the routine eventually settled into my being and the daily gatherings became a normal pace of existence. The struggles of clarifying Church teachings and disciplines, and the interweavings – if not contradictions – of varying traditions and ways of life, soon called on all my energies and required my total attention. I have never expended more energy than I did during the four sessions of Vatican II. My contacts with the several renewal movements that had been stirring before the Council had prepared me somewhat for what was happening. And my respect for the person and the leadership of Pope John XXIII soon led me to embrace his vision and thank God for having called me to this wonderful new understanding of what my faith was all about.

My sense of the movement of the Holy Spirit kept growing as the pace of the Council unfolded. There were indeed periods of high tension, hours of depression when efforts at renewal seemed to falter, but also times of great elation and joyous response to what I felt was indeed a prophetic venture. Never in my whole life have I been more proud of being a Catholic than during those heady and historic days.

A Day at the Council

Ecumenical Councils are rare events. Only 21 have been recognized in the history of the Catholic Church. The early ones were in the Eastern World, and several were convened by Emperors, but not by the Latin Patriarch in Rome. Mostly these councils aimed to combat heresies or clarify points of theology or discipline. Vatican II was an exception, as there were no specific heresies to be condemned: Pope John XXIII was very clear on this point. Some people have been tempted to downgrade the Council because it was not "doctrinally" focused. I like to recall that Jesus identified himself not only as "Truth" but also as "Way" and "Life." Vatican II concerned itself with the full spectrum of Catholic life and simultaneously reached out to the entire world. Hence I see doctrine as embracing the totality of the human. *Gaudium et Spes* ("joys and hopes"), the document on the Church in the Modern World, presents Jesus Christ as the model or prototype of the New Human (GS 22). This to me is broader and more substantial than doctrinal precision. Our hearts and bodies are included, as well as our minds. Vatican II offered us invaluable guidance to prepare us for the new millennium we have just entered. The general themes and principles found in the first section of *Gaudium et Spes* are well worth rereading from this perspective.

In my case, since canonical jurisdiction accompanied my nomination as Ordinary of the Diocese of Victoria, I was advised to assume without delay my responsibility, and to represent my newly acquired diocese at the Council, thus beginning to serve the people of Vancouver Island even before I was ordained bishop in Saint Boniface on December 14, 1962, and installed at Saint Andrew's Cathedral in Victoria on December 20. Rising early each morning at the General Headquarters of the Marianist Brothers on the Via Latina, where I was boarding, I would start my usual spiritual exercises, have breakfast with my associates and find my seat in one of the cars at our disposal for the 20-minute trip to Saint Peter's Basilica. The Council was primarily a liturgical celebration, so Eucharist was the first thing on the agenda. It was initially presided over by one bishop from any one of the over 20 rites that are in active communion with Rome. These spring from five original Patriarchates (Jerusalem, Antioch, Alexandria, Constantinople and Rome). The Council awakened many of the Latin Rite faithful to the fact that the Latin Rite, which presently has the most members, owes its initial recognition to leaders of the Eastern world.

After the Eucharist, the Sacred Scriptures, in the form of a richly adorned Lectionary, were enthroned for the veneration of all in attendance. The book was incensed and surrounded with candles. This provided us with a daily reminder that the "real presence" has a variety of forms, as we would later proclaim in our Council teachings. It is worth recalling that an Ecumenical Council is primarily an act of worship, and that the entire Church stands under the light of Revelation. This is a far cry from the sociological interpretation that the mass media so frequently attributed to the Council, considering it as a debating club or reporting mainly on events that had a controversial component or angle.

After this time of veneration of the Word, the Council Fathers got down to the business of the day. Generally, this meant receiving some pertinent information about topics and procedures. Then followed the speeches, normally limited to ten minutes. Discipline in this regard was strict, with very few exceptions allowed. The sessions terminated at 1:00 p.m. Then everyone promptly moved out into the Plaza on their way home to lunch and siesta. The late afternoon and evening were occupied with consultations, study, meetings and sometimes late-night gatherings for strategy sessions and the drafting of presentations for the next day. Speakers – with the exception of the Cardinals, who could ask for the floor when they saw fit – had to give advance notice.

It was not long before the Assembly tired of hearing monologues and sometimes repetitious "interventions" from individual speakers. It was eventually agreed that Council Fathers who spoke in the name of a group would be prioritized in the speakers' list. Written remarks could be submitted at any time. Of course this meant lots of backstage work to get lists of signatures indicating a speaker had widespread support.

During the closed-door sessions, sharp or very critical statements were occasionally proffered. But very rarely were any words spoken in hostility, and even then they arose out of a dedicated and honest search for truth. The struggle between the truth and the ego can be difficult! Etched in my memory are the tone and intensity with which the then Abbott of Downside Abbey, Christopher Butler, O.S.B., later auxiliary bishop of Westminster, addressed the Assembly. When Butler spoke, we listened! He rejected the negative things that some bishops had said about scholars (and theologians!) and simply raised the question "Ne timeamus quod veritas veritati noceat!" (We should not fear that truth might somehow tell against truth!) This phrase has stayed with me and continues to remind me of the need to keep pursuing truth even, and perhaps especially, when it becomes difficult or inconvenient.

Even during the dark hours referred to by some commentators as the "black week" of November 16, 1964, when there was notable tension between the bishops and Pope Paul VI, I do not recall having heard any words that were deliberately offensive. I did learn how hard truths can be painful for prophets and hearers alike, yet necessary for the promotion of the Reign of God.

I personally addressed the Council on four occasions, with a number of bishops co-signing. I also submitted and signed over a dozen written observations. One of these was the formal request for the restoration in the Latin Rite of the form of dedicated life known as the eremitic, or "hermit," state. This was granted and is now incorporated in the revised Code of Canon Law (#603). A direct result of this restoration was the establishing of an experimental colony of hermits on Vancouver Island in 1964. Several monks from a variety of religious communities wanted to join together with a Benedictine abbot, Dom Jacques Winandy, in living the hermetic life. These men were previously experienced religious who chose to live singly and in total solitude, normally in a remote area. The hermetic calling is unique and their regime of life is severely disciplined, a witness to the "divine absolute." I later ordained one of them, Charles Brandt, as a diocesan priest and a local witness to this form of life. The diocese thus acquired the distinction of being the site of the restoration in the Western world of the previously interrupted hermetical tradition, which has remained fairly common in the Eastern churches, and was now once again made possible through the work of the Vatican Council.

The Council Fathers had to maintain a rigorous schedule. It eventually took its toll in terms of weariness and health problems for some of the elderly or more frail participants. Thank God, at age 38 that was no problem for me. But I know that several lives ended prematurely by the willing sacrifice of these dedicated pastors. Imagine yourself, already loaded down with heavy schedules and countless concerns, having to set aside, for four years, well over two months of your time. Or coming home to your people and trying to explain why you were now thinking so differently, attempting to share a new vision despite the normal, sometimes intense and less than favourable reactions of astonished people. And for those bishops who really caught the prophetic mood that developed out of Pope John XXIII's vision, this really meant running two full-time agendas simultaneously. For some of us, this started back in 1959, when the Cardinal Secretary of State, writing in the Pope's name, invited all the bishops of the world to prepare, and to send to the appropriate Pontifical Commission lists of suggestions for the agenda of the forthcoming council.

An Ecumenical Council is the highest authority in the Catholic Church. Its ultimate status in history is subject to its "reception" by the People of God in its entirety. Vatican II helped us tremendously in this regard by formally addressing, for the first time in history, the question "Church, who are you?" How the Holy Spirit continues to animate, enlighten and guide the Church on its pilgrim journey towards the Reign of God remains both a mystery and a source of admiration for all believers. Before Vatican II we did not have a proper theology of the Church, an ecclesiology; rather, we had a hierarchology, focused primarily on the bishops, with little concern for the entire *laos* or people of God.

Vatican II reversed the order in which we approached Catholic doctrine. We used to start with apologetics (defending our teachings and current Catholic practices). These we then shored up with Canon Law, mostly do's and don'ts, defending our orthodoxy against those who were in error. Lastly, we had recourse to Scripture, often by selective "proof texting" (using Scripture selectively to back up our opinions) to assure ourselves that we were right and our adversaries were wrong.

Today we start from Revelation, the fullness of which we recognize in the person of Jesus Christ our Redeemer. Faith is thus primarily a relationship instead of a list of doctrines. Then we use theology to elucidate Tradition, which is the living interpretation of the Sacred Scriptures along with the writings themselves. Creative theologians help us grow spiritually by finding or developing language that helps us understand more deeply the mysterious saving design of God. I am greatly indebted to all the theologians who have helped me to discern the signs of the times. Lastly, we use Canon Law as a necessary guide to channel the energies of the Body of Christ here on earth. There must be salutary order to keep the variety and diversity of ministries working together towards unity in harmony. This is obviously an oversimplification of complex interwoven beliefs and disciplines. But it does illustrate further how profoundly our current faith life has been enriched and clarified by Vatican II. We are only beginning to appreciate more fully what this all means for our pastoral life as members of the Church.

There has probably never been a Church gathering of this magnitude. Well over 2,500 bishops from around the world participated and worked very hard for at least four years – some considerably longer. They were assisted by over a hundred scholars, most of whom held doctorates in their respective disciplines. Add a long list of Observers from other churches or faiths and you have an idea of the brain power involved. There was further global outreach in the multiple consultations with universities and other sites of higher learning. The phenomenon of such a huge gathering in Rome may never be seen again. Someone compared the sight of all these bishops emerging at 1:00 p.m. from St. Peter's to that of a river of purple flowing down from the Basilica into the Via della Conciliazione. Considering the cost in terms of human energy and economics, plus the availability of modern electronic communications, such a process may well be considered obsolete today. It also occurred to me during the proceedings that the format and process were not the most effective or productive. Modern psychology and pedagogical methods would counsel the use of a better and less expensive way to obtain equal or even better results. As the saying goes, hindsight is always 20/20.

Observers at the Council

Any description of Vatican II would be incomplete if it did not mention the presence of Observers from other churches and faith traditions. The Observers were not entitled to speak, but they had translators available to explain all the official documents. Meaningful friendships were also established and serious conversations ensued, resulting in very constructive suggestions being transmitted to the Commission leaders. Their observations were gratefully received and treated with much deference. I made friends with several of the Observers and kept in touch with a few of them for years afterwards.

I am thoroughly convinced that Vatican II was the fruit of a special inspiration. Blessed John XXIII repeatedly indicated that the idea came to him by divine inspiration. His successors in the Chair of Peter have added their positive assessment to his. The special Synod of Bishops convened in 1985 to review the results of the Council declared that Vatican II was indeed a prophetic happening, a beacon of hope and light for the future.

But Vatican II has also met with strenuous opposition from powerful and determined groups of people. History tells us we should not be unduly surprised. Students of social dynamics warn us that momentous events generate upheavals and resistance. Change is rarely welcomed by people who are accustomed to, and profit from, the status quo.

I also believe that our attitude towards or resistance to the movements of the Holy Spirit are a factor in all this. In fact, this might be an indication of the lack of an adequate theology of the Holy Spirit, or one that has atrophied or not become sufficiently developed. "By their fruits you will know them," affirms the Bible. As I continue to travel and share my experience of Vatican II, I am both saddened and simultaneously amazed. I am saddened to learn how little is known about Vatican II even 50 years later. It seems many of our clerical leaders have chosen not to speak about the Council, or have opted out of its vision. Yet I remain hopeful and joyous – amazed, even – because I constantly meet more and more people who cling to the vision of John XXIII, are praying for its realization, and are engaged in creative projects that spread its message of hope.

It would be a serious misunderstanding, resulting in needless confusion, to oppose the authority of a Council and of the Pope. A council includes the Pope as well as all the bishops in communion with Rome, and can only be legitimately celebrated when convened or at least approved by the Bishop of Rome. The precise point of whether Pope or Council can supersede each other is still open and may well not be brought to resolution for a long time to come. Let us concentrate our energies on living pastoral issues rather than on theoretical considerations.

*

As a young priest, I had never dwelled on the thought that I might someday become a bishop, even though friends had, on a few occasions, teased me about it. I was content to be in parish ministry, for I enjoyed its challenges, and felt I had sufficient responsibility already. I had observed several bishops spending themselves relentlessly and did not envy them in the least.

However, once I had recovered from the shock of my unexpected appointment, I told a friend that if God wanted me in the college of bishops, this was the best possible time to begin a new era, with the celebration of a Council. When I read the opening address of Pope John XXIII at the inauguration, which saw the Council rising in the Church like a new daybreak, I was deeply moved. As his vision began to awaken and stir in my consciousness, I became elated. And my first encounter with him at the papal audience in mid-November warmed my heart. It convinced me that I was called to work with a truly prophetic person, a visionary as well as a saint. The memory of that event will remain with me as long as I live. To mark my attendance as the youngest Canadian bishop at the Council, Pope John referred to me as "our Benjamin" and presented me with a ring.

After the Council, I habitually shared Pope John's ring with many people. Many venerated it like a relic, particularly after his beatification. Less frequently, I also let interested people try a second ring, which Pope Paul VI gifted to all the bishops towards the closing of the Council. These rings brought both pleasure and spiritual encouragement to a great many people. Sad to say, I ignored the warnings of friends who cautioned me about losing them. Somehow, the rings ceased to come back to me. Did I misplace them? Did someone feel they were entitled to keep them? I hope and pray that someday they will be found and returned to me. Pope John's ring is square and holds a large, rather pale amethyst. Inside there is a clip, which once was required because bishops wore gloves and the clip would prevent the ring from sliding off his finger when the gloves were removed. Pope Paul's ring is a plain gold one, shaped like a bishop's mitre, embossed with three figures: Christ, Peter and Paul. Neither of these rings has great commercial value, but their sentimental value to me is beyond price.

Media and Women at the Council

During the sessions of the Council, reporters and other media representatives played a crucial role at Vatican II. Many of them somehow overcame the official "strictures" imposed on them, such as "pontifical secrecy," and had access to reliable information rather than highly filtered reports. I know for a fact that the Canadian bishops were among the first to facilitate the sharing of reliable information. Thanks in good part to the media, the entire world followed the unfolding of the Council. Our Manitoba team set the example by providing regular radio and printed messages destined for the people in Canada.

One reporter, Bonnie Brennan, endeared herself to all the bishops of Canada. She was a highly skilled worker in the burgeoning world of modern mass media. She served the Canadian bishops' conference with exemplary dedication for many years. Together with the Paulist Father Frank Stone, she also assisted the cause of ecumenism in Toronto and across North America. She and Bernard Daly formed our English-speaking press team in Rome and were very active as members of the press throughout the Council. Robert Blair Kaiser, an American journalist with *Time* magazine, was also very influential in bringing the Council and its impact to the attention of the world.

During the Council's second session, it dawned on me that it would be very useful for Bonnie to spend some time inside St. Peter's during the deliberations so she could get a better feel for its workings and process. Access to St. Peter's during the official sittings required a special passport. (The presence of women would be allowed only later, during the third session.) In consultation with a few other bishops, I devised a plan whereby Bonnie might also receive a passport. I drew up a petition to that effect on formal letterhead and had it signed by a large number of other bishops, who gladly acquiesced. I often wondered what went on in the Vatican Council protocol section when the request reached the office!

I eventually obtained the document. Imagine my surprise when I saw the title on the passport: "Rev. Sacerdote Bonnie Brennan." Was that how the official in charge saved face? He certainly knew it was technically against the rules, but how could one refuse a request from a substantial group of bishops who had authority at the Council? Archbishop Maurice Baudoux roared with laughter when he saw it. Many others joined in the merriment and paid their solemn respects to her. Bonnie enjoyed her day at the Council. But the merriment over this incident was short-lived. The General Secretary Archbishop Pericle Felici got wind of the situation and personally intervened, promptly confiscating the document.

In fact, the question of the official ministries of women was not on the agenda for the Council. It was taken for granted at the time that women were not entitled to exercise authority in the Church in any official capacity. Cardinal Leo Josef Suenens of Belgium was one of the first to raise that issue, reminding us that women constitute the majority of Church membership. But much of that way of thinking fell on deaf ears. The time was not yet ripe. However, a small but resolute group of women, centred in the St. Joan's Alliance, was very active in Rome, raising several pertinent issues with a number of Council Fathers, and indirectly exercising considerable influence. In addition there was the British economist Barbara Ward. She was held in such high esteem that a request was made for her to be allowed to speak, and she prepared a paper on poverty and hunger. However, the secretary-general discovered that the "B. Ward" on his list was a woman, which could not be allowed. A compromise was reached by having her paper read in Latin by an auditor, a layman, Jim Norris, deputy director of the Catholic Relief Services. During the third session, several women were officially appointed as "Auditores," allowed to be present at the sessions but without speaking privileges.

Vatican II never addressed the question of the possibility of ordaining women. It was not on the agenda. But some years back, I made a statement to the effect that the question of the future ministries of women in the Church was of such importance that it called for the communal discernment of the entire people of God, not just the hierarchy. The results were predictable. This was one of several times I have been censured in one way or another. Be that as it may, I remember clearly Dominican Father Yves Congar, who was appointed a Cardinal before his death, and one of the most renowned scholars I have known, telling a gathering of the Canadian bishops that with respect to the specific issue of women's ordination, one could not make a meaningful argument one way or the other on the basis of Sacred Scripture alone. It is an entirely new issue, not foreseen before Vatican II. I remain convinced that censorship is not the best approach to contentious issues in the Church. Will we ever learn the lesson of Gamaliel (see Acts 5.34-39)? We are dealing with the emerging Reign of God. That which is not truly of divine inspiration will ultimately fade away. Salutary truth will prevail in the end. We must all pray ardently for the guidance of the Holy Spirit as we move into the future.

The presence of women at the sessions awakens in me another delightful recollection. Pope John XXIII was sensitive enough to matters human to realize that most bishops, particularly the older or somewhat frail members and those not fluent in Latin, would find it unbearable to be consigned to relatively hard seats while listening to an extended series of 10-minute monologues. He gave instructions that a "bar" be installed in one of the nearby corridors. It dispensed a variety of refreshments and afforded limited space for bishops to meet and to discuss current issues. That bar was almost immediately flooded with people, and a second one was soon required. Later on, in the third session, with women attending, the Italian sense of propriety kicked in and a third bar was provided as well, intended for the women.

Now, the question arose: how to tell someone where you could meet for a conversation? How to identify which bar would serve as the appropriate meeting place? Three names began to circulate and soon became common currency. The original bar was given the name of "Bar Jonah," in honor of Pope Giovanni. Bar number two was situated on the mezzanine level, near the gathered Superiors General of men's orders and the Abbots. So, why not call it "Bar Abbas"? The third one, for the women, presented no problem. The General Secretary had instructed us that the women's bar was off limits to us men. However, he somehow did not share this admonition with the women. They proved to have no hesitation in inviting bishops to meet them at the women's bar: "Bar Nun (None?)."

A. De Roo family farm, built in the 1920s, located almost 4 miles northwest of Swan Lake, Manitoba. Remi and his seven siblings were born here.

B. First Communion day for Remi and his brother Michael, summer of 1929.
From left: sister Gerarda, mother Josephine, baby Clara, Remi, Michael, father Raymond.

A. Remi in 1944, age 20, after his second year at St. Boniface College,
a Catholic and French-speaking affiliate of the University of Manitoba.

B. Semi-private audience with Pope Pius XII, August 1958. Remi is standing third from left.
On his left are Judith Stangl and Joanne (in front) Stangl, and their parents, Joseph C.
and Katherine Stangl, friends from Holy Cross Parish, Norwood, Manitoba.
(Others in photo are an unidentified group of pilgrims.)

A. Episcopal ordination banquet, December 14, 1962, with Archbishop Maurice Baudoux of St. Boniface, presiding Prelate, and Remi's father, Raymond.

B. Ring of Pope John XXIII, presented via Cardinal Léger and sent to Remi as the Canadian "Benjamin" in November 1962, the day after his audience with the Canadian bishops attending the Second Vatican Council.

C. Remi as Bishop-elect of Victoria, November 1962, holding the bejewelled pectoral cross entrusted to him by the Archdiocese of St. Boniface, where he served prior to his appointment.

A. Bishop Remi (right) with unidentified Italian brother bishop during opening morning prayer, "Adsumus," at a regular daily session of the Council, 1963. Each day began with the celebration of Eucharist and enthronement of a special Book of the Gospels.

B. Bishop Remi in 1989 with United Church Presbytery Officer Reverend William Howie (centre) and Anglican Bishop of B.C. Ronald Shepherd at Nootka, B.C., for the 200th anniversary celebrations of Spanish missionaries' arrival on Vancouver Island.

C. Bishops at a Solemn Session of the Vatican Council, vested in ceremonial copes for proclamations. The circle in the right middle section identifies Bishop Remi.

A. Remi De Roo's Installation as 14th Bishop of the Diocese of Vancouver Island, December 20, 1962. The crozier belonged to his predecessor, Bishop James Michael Hill, and was later replaced by a standard wooden shepherd's crook.

A. Bishop Remi erecting a cross with a representative of the Native Peoples, Chief Ed Underwood, at the Tsawout East Saanich Indian Reserve, February 14, 1963. The first cross was planted nearby by Bishop Modeste Demers at his arrival in 1852.

B. Bishop Remi is draped in a ceremonial blanket by two Native women during the official seating at his initiation ceremony in the longhouse. He was adopted into the First Nations race and given the name "Siem LePleet S'HWUWQUN," Great High Priest White Swan.

A. Welcomed on board by the Captain of the destroyer *Beacon Hill* on June 3, 1963, along with Archbishop Harold Sexton, en route to viewing military exercises, passage to Tofino, B.C., and descent by piping at the dock.

B. February 14, 1963. The Sahale Stick, topped with a thunderbird (representing the Holy Spirit) carved from a tree branch. The stick was used by early missionaries to teach religion, using its carved notches to represent historical periods.

A. As this editorial cartoon suggests, Bishop Remi boarded countless flights out of Victoria to give lectures or participate in various activities in Canada and around the world.

B. Family gathering, Summer 1973, Swan Lake, Manitoba.
From left: Clara, Remi, Gerarda, Madeline, Cyril, Raymond, Michael, Alma, Marguerite.

A. Bishop Remi laying hands on Terry McNamara, OMI, at his ordination
to the ministerial priesthood amid Native ceremonies in the Quamichan longhouse,
Tzouhalem Road, Duncan, B.C., July 15, 1979.

B. International Apostleship of the Sea Congress, Rome, September 1975,
meeting Pope Paul VI with Cardinal Sebastiano Baggio, former Apostolic Delegate
to Canada and Prefect of the Congregation of Bishops in Rome.

A. Bishop Remi hosted by Henry Smith (holding blanket) and unidentified host at the Holy Week Good Friday service in the Malahat longhouse, 1978.

© Felici, Rome.

B. Bishop Remi presenting documents pertaining to the Victoria Diocesan Synod of 1986–1992 to Pope John Paul II at the Vatican, Summer 1993.

A. Bishop Remi as co-chair of the Social Affairs Commission of the Canadian Conference of Catholic Bishops, speaking with representatives of the mass media, 1983.

B. Bishop Remi enjoying a light moment with his friend the Canadian journalist Roy Bonisteel (host of CBC TV's *Man Alive* from 1967 to 1989) at the 1977 Convention in Vancouver, B.C., of the Catholic Health Association of Canada.

A. Bishop Remi at Koinonia bookstore, Victoria, in 1992, signing a copy of
In the Eye of the Catholic Storm as owner Judy Ravai and customers look on.

DEZE EERSTE STEEN
WERD GEWIJD DOOR
Z.H.EXC.MGR.REMI DE ROO
BISSCHOP VAN
VICTORIA B. C.(CANADA)
15 SEPT. 1963

B. Bishop Remi on a visit to Lembeke, East Flanders, Belgium, the birthplace of his parents,
beside the cornerstone of the parish centre, which he blessed on September 15, 1963,
en route to the Second Vatican Council.

A. Bishop Remi with Brother Roger Schutz, founder of the Taizé Community, at Taizé, France, shortly before Brother Roger's death in 2005.

B. Bishop Remi presiding at Eucharist for the wedding of Ray Seller and Muriel Hanman at Bethlehem Retreat Centre Chapel, Nanaimo, B.C., September 26, 2009.

A. Bishop Remi receiving an Honorary Doctor of Laws degree at Brandon University
Convocation, Manitoba, May 23, 1987, with Dean of Arts Peter Hordern.
This was one of five honorary degrees he received
(Antigonish, Toronto Ryerson Institute, Winnipeg, Brandon, and Victoria).

B. In Lembeke, Belgium, in the 1980s, reconnecting with descendants of Meil Geirnaert,
who had worked for Remi's father in Swan Lake, Manitoba, before returning to Belgium.

A. Concelebrating the Eucharist with Bishop Aloysius Jin of Shanghai during a pilgrimage at the renowned Chinese Marian Shrine of Our Lady of Sheshan, May 1, 2008. Bishop Remi was invited on two occasions to give a series of lectures about Vatican II to seminarians and religious in the Shanghai Diocese.

B. De Roo international family reunion at Oostakker in Belgium, August 24, 2008, with participants from several countries. Remi is in the front row, fourth from right. There were 376 family members present. Thirty-seven came from Canada, the United States, Portugal, France, Spain, Germany, Switzerland, Brazil and The Netherlands. In 2005, a similar reunion of the De Pape side of the family was held near Ghent, Belgium.

A. Bishop Remi with long-time friend Senator Douglas Roche, O.C.,
who co-authored *Man to Man* and *In the Eye of the Catholic Storm* (with Mary Jo Leddy),
enjoying a moment of relaxation during work on these Chronicles, January 2012.

B. Bishop Remi with Diane Tolomeo and Pearl Gervais at the launching of their book,
Biblical Characters and the Enneagram, January 2001.

3

VATICAN II IN A NUTSHELL

As a child, I learned my catechism by heart. I can still recite some of its formulas. It was primarily an intellectual exercise and had little to do with what I felt in my heart or did with my body. I do not recall much emphasis being placed on how I should live or behave, other than to "be good!" It was primarily head stuff. Such was my experience. I believe it portrays a former way of life for many devout and admirable people.

My seminary studies, although appropriate for the times, were also focused on a narrow theology and inadequate scripture courses, a morality of precepts and obligations, structured prayer, obedience, loyalty and aspects of Church legislation. Out of these times, the Second Vatican Council did not appear suddenly on the horizon. Already, in those earlier days, many believers were starting to realize that life could not continue along this road if one were to have a vibrant faith based not only on Jesus' expression of "I am the Truth," but also of the rest of his sentence: "I am the Way, the Truth, and the Life." What way? What life? How would those elements be lived with just the practice of believing? The questions being asked with great love and concern were silently fomenting into one graced and inspired moment when Pope John XXIII called the Second Vatican Council in 1961.

The times were bleak: the world seemed on the brink of destruction. Technology had advanced greatly, but so had secularism. Was the Church losing its way? Was it, too, wondering about its mission to inspire and promote truth and peace? John XXIII was hearing pessimistic voices about the state of the world. He heard blame about modern times bringing on a deterioration of morals and truth. But the Pope disagreed with the prophets of doom and gloom. "The human family is on the threshold of a new era," he said in his opening remarks to the Council in October 1962. He went on to ask the Council Fathers to see the hand of God ever directing people's efforts, "whether they realize it or not, towards the fulfillment of the inscrutable designs of His providence, wisely arranging everything, even adverse human fortune, for the Church's good."

Rather than addressing errors in doctrine or heresies, this Council would reach out in pastoral ways to the needs of a renewed Church and society, injecting new joy, new enthusiasm and serenity of mind. All people in a rapidly moving world were deserving of such encouragement, of guidance, of evocative challenge, and of support in strengthening their spirituality.

Pope John's faith in the Spirit kindled my own faith. What an exciting era! Jesus had promised that he would be with us for all time, and Pope John wished to reaffirm that basic tenet. He called the Church to ask itself, "Who are you?" and "Given the wisdom of Scripture, of Tradition and of the abiding presence of God, what is your mission in today's world?"

Thus began the pastoral Council of Vatican II. Thus for me began my life as a bishop already a member of the People of God. I, too, was prompted to answer the question, "Remi, who are you and what is your mission in this new world?" I was not alone. Some 2,500 other bishops had also, for the most part, learned a theology that was largely academic, whose pastoral implications for ministry were somewhat secondary. Here we were, shepherds of a flock, learning, listening and struggling to trace a trajectory of a new way of being pastors, revisiting the body of theology in renewed and pastoral ways. Up to this point, the Church was defined as an institution that held all the sacred truths.

And here we stood, despite our differences, united in one intent: to renew ourselves and our Church, and to share that new vision with all who might listen. It was indeed true that at times we would need the serenity of mind, a spirit of brotherly concord, moderation in our proposals, dignity in discussion, and wisdom in deliberation of which John XXIII had reminded us in his speech at the opening of the Council. This became the most meaningful and challenging experience of grace for me, a bishop – and a very young one at that. To offer you a nutshell summary of Vatican II, its meaning and its heritage, is to cull what for me are the major themes from which all others flow.

The bishops and their assistants came from all over the globe. They represented a vast array of cultures and perspectives, although the Western influence was still predominant in many ways. For instance, the primary focus of religious scholars in our Western world is on orthodoxy (correct teaching) and orthopraxis (appropriate conduct). For those who grow up in the Eastern cultures, though, the emphasis tends to be on harmony, on correct relationships, on getting along together. Many of us, though we were not familiar with Eastern customs, tried to reach out to our brother bishops from other Rites. I learned a lot from them. I was particularly enriched by having known and worked with an outstanding leader of the Ukrainian Church, the Metropolitan for all of Canada, Archeparch Maxime Hermaniuk. He was a very influential voice in the debate on collegiality. The Eastern Rites have always retained the practice of church government through the synods. Vatican II was considered in some ways a balancing act to correct the heavy accent placed on papal authority by the first Vatican Council in 1869–1870, which was never fully terminated. In fact, the first thing Blessed Pope John XXIII did was to formally close Vatican I before opening Vatican II!

Ressourcement, Aggiornamento and Development

I can think of no better way to share what Vatican II declared than to recall the three words that summarize it best: *ressourcement*, *aggiornamento* and development. These terms describe the process that guided the Council's discussions. I dare say they are terms that we would be wise to continue to use.

Ressourcement is a French word that speaks of going back to our earliest sources to reclaim the basic teachings Jesus gave to his disciples, which were eventually formulated as doctrines or traditions. The scholars took us back to sources within Scripture and Tradition. We saw the Church defined in Scripture as the vineyard where all are invited to work, and as the field in which hidden treasures wait to be found. We recalled that we are branches bonded to Jesus the vine, the source of life, and grafted to the ancient tree of our Jewish heritage. Scripture came alive, and the daily recitation of my breviary took on new meaning beyond the simple fulfillment of a "spiritual duty."

Through my seminary days, spirituality was perceived as primarily composed of exercises and practices. The Commandments played a key role. The Beatitudes were mentioned on occasion but were not considered as central to spiritual growth. Vatican II brought about a real change, a conversion, almost a revolution in my spiritual life. Rather than conditions to be fulfilled to obtain a place in heaven, my spirituality started to feel more like partnership with Jesus Christ on a pilgrimage through the Paschal Mystery, sharing his death, resurrection and imparting of the Holy Spirit. One of the central experiences that brought about this change was the concelebration of the Eucharist with all the bishops – Eastern and Western – assembled in St. Peter's. It was almost like a preview of heaven to feel the energy vibrating through this impressive international body of Church leaders praying together with our formerly "separate" brothers, participating in the same mystery of salvation. The enthronement of the Bible placed us in the constant presence of the Word of God. Somehow all the petty local considerations dropped off to give way to a deep sense of the sacred and the mystic. For the first time, I sensed the full implications as we said the prayer over the offerings: "Every time these sacred mysteries are celebrated the work of our redemption is accomplished."

Before the Council, the mention of "Church" commonly evoked an image of buildings, the Pope, the bishops and priests, and maybe the nuns. It was a vertical model, with each level having its own tasks. The bottom level, over 90 percent of the faithful, existed to "pray, pay and obey." Ordinary folk needed the Church mainly to get to heaven. But

Vatican II popularized the image of the Church as a pilgrim people, journeying in the midst of history, at once holy and yet always in need of purification. With that view goes the acknowledgement that history also plays a role in the unfolding of the Reign of God – not only within the Church, but in the whole of creation as well. In earlier days, I do not recall having heard very much said from church pulpits about the Reign of God. Yet the Gospel makes a point of indicating that the divine Kingdom is at the very core of the Good News that Jesus brought into the world, and the very Person of Jesus constitutes the Good News itself. It was a major shift from the earlier image of the Church as a fortress on the hill, demanding honour, power and blind obedience.

As well, the reclaiming of the doctrine of the local church affirmed that the Church of Christ is truly present in all legitimate local faith groups. Parents are invited to see themselves as the first preachers of the faith, by word and example, in what the Council calls the domestic church, or the home. As Pope John said at the very first session, the Church is the "loving mother of all," spreading everywhere the fullness of Christian charity.

Going back to our sources also meant reclaiming some elements of the administrative side of the Church. One area in which this process is found is in the basic concept of subsidiarity (as understood and proposed by John XXIII), which also embraces synodality and collegiality. The principles are clear, but they are more frequently recognized in the breach than in their application. This is particularly true regarding the local churches and the full powers bestowed in the sacrament of episcopal ordination. Judging from recent tensions in that area, it often seems that we have experienced more reversal than progress in applying this major tenet of Vatican II.

The same holds true for parish life: in all my travels, I have witnessed ongoing problems around what appears to be a power struggle. More than once I have winced at the painful stories of generous volunteers who have been reprimanded, disempowered or harassed by immature leaders, ordained or lay, because they were seen as infringing on the territory or privileges claimed by the one in charge. Vatican II repeated almost *ad nauseam* the instruction that ministry is meant to be service to fellow believers, rather than power over them.

While *ressourcement* looked back to our past, *aggiornamento* looked ahead to our future renewal. Pope John offered us this direction in his opening remarks to the Council: "For this deposit of faith, or truths that are contained in our time-honored teaching, is one thing; the manner in which these truths are set forth (with their meaning preserved intact) is something else." We were invited to recall that the people of God, in communion with their bishop, who is the symbol and agent of unity, constitute a local church assembly in which the full church is mysteriously but truly present. Indeed, the Council emphasized the startling declaration that the whole anointed people cannot be mistaken in belief. It may not always feel that way, but we need to remember that bishops, priests and assembly together participate in this truth.

We were prompted to answer the universal call to holiness, by which all the baptized are meant to progress in holiness, even to become mystics, as Jesus told us to "be perfect as my Father is perfect" (Matt. 5.48). This may be a good place to insert what Vatican II taught me about faith. I said earlier that my previous understanding of faith was the assent of the mind to a series of propositions. Vatican II returned to a more biblically based understanding. I now understand faith as more than a set of intellectual assertions: it is the relationship of my total being to God in, with and through Jesus the Christ. With love and joy, as a child to a parent, one trusts and freely commits one's entire self to God "by the obedience of faith." Compare this with the earlier Vatican I wording, in which "full obedience of intellect and will" says nothing about our hearts or total physical selves.

Some have referred to Vatican II as Cardinal Newman's council; when I use the term *development*, I am borrowing a word from Newman's essay, written a century earlier, on the development of doctrine. Newman asserted that it was normal for the Church throughout history to elaborate and expand on its original teachings. He also stressed the need for consultation with all the faithful as a guarantee of orthodoxy. Church teachings come alive and become truly effective through their reception by the entire body of believers. To speak of "development" in the Council was to admit that we did not have all the answers to the questions our flocks were asking. It is hard to believe that this was a new concept! In fact, Cardinal Alfredo Ottaviani had as his episcopal motto *Semper idem* (Always the same).

Our work was to convey an invitation to live the Beatitudes rather than formulate more legislation to induce further conformity. Appropriate renewal was brought to many domains. We refocused the Church on the Person of Jesus Christ rather than on the external structures of a "perfect society" in which we took pride. The previous emphasis, as I recall from my youth, seemed to attribute more importance to individual devotions and pious practices (such as saying personal prayers or reciting the Rosary during the Mass, which was perceived as a performance by the priest in the Latin language very few people could understand).

In my own experiences of long waits, words and walks, I am more and more convinced that in our day and age, we hurry and do not allow the fullness of wisdom to unfold. The document on Divine Revelation (*Dei Verbum*) had a very long birthing. Like any enduring piece of art, it took patience, skill and time to mature. If you participate in a Bible study group, or prepare faith reflections on Scripture readings, you have likely been greatly influenced by this document. It encouraged the reading of Scripture to discover what is revealed in what might be hidden in both the Hebrew and the Christian writings. St. Jerome stated that "ignorance of the Scriptures is ignorance of Christ"; we are encouraged to immerse ourselves in them, to read, discuss, pray and meditate over them, and then to take action.

Before Vatican II, Protestants and Catholics were locked in controversy over the relationship between the Scriptures and the Magisterium (teaching office) of the Church. It was like a dialogue of the deaf. The Council spoke of these "two Sources" of Revelation, but went on to say that Revelation did not originate in either the Bible or the Magisterium: it came to us through the Person of Jesus Christ. He is both the messenger and the message. The entire revelation of the Gospel is summed up in the Person of Jesus Christ. God's plan of revelation is thereby realized in both deeds and words.

Added to this, we can understand our own tradition better by regarding the Magisterium as the servant of the word. This supremacy that *Dei Verbum* attributed to the Sacred Scriptures has helped to set the stage for progress in ecumenism. All the baptized are called to study, meditate on and pray with Scripture, the "soul of theology."

One of my regrets is that the Council did not provide more indepth presentations about the Sacred Scriptures. Biblical scholarship was just recovering from a time of neglect. Pope Pius XII had opened doors that had been shut tight during the strictures placed on what was then known as "modernism." His encyclical *Divino Afflante Spiritu* helped restore freedom for Catholic biblical scholarship.

However, it took Blessed Pope John XXIII to invite a number of formerly silenced scholars to the Council to begin anew to share the fruits of their labours with the Council Fathers. Had more of them been active at the Council, I believe we would have been substantially enriched. This pertains especially to the questions of ordination of mature married men, the place of women in the Church, and the variety of ministries that might be officially entrusted to them. Even a cursory reading of 1 Corinthians makes it clear that women shared equally with men in proclaiming the Good News and in ministering in a variety of functions.

A Pastoral Council

Vatican II was a pastoral Council. It had practical implementations in worship, preaching, adult faith development, catechetics and social action. During my time as an active bishop, I reminded the ordained ministers that the homily was to be a reflection on the Word of God as proclaimed that day rather than a treatise on some other topic. Even though we do not always have ready answers for questions raised by scriptural readings, we must not fall back into didactic responses to complex questions. Periodically, like many others, I wonder, what *would* Jesus do or say in a particular instance?

For me, one of the most meaningful documents to come out of the Council is *Lumen Gentium* (Light of All Nations). This document answers the question of "Church, who are you?" We Council Fathers, by a large majority, had heard our communities calling for renewal, mercy and truth. One of the key teachings of *Lumen Gentium* is the image of the People of God, chosen by divine initiative, not just as separate individuals but as a community, with Christ as its Head, already here on earth offering a seed of unity, hope and salvation for all humankind and the entire cosmos. We reminded ourselves that servant-leadership needs to replace domination or power. The vertical and hierarchical development that, through the centuries, had shaped the governing Church institutions into a pyramid of power was cautiously redirected towards the more primitive and traditional image of the circle.

For the first time ever, an Ecumenical Council recognized the rights of all the baptized. The laity have the right and sometimes the duty to express their opinions on matters pertaining to the common good, and pastors should leave them freedom and scope for activity. This effective recognition is for me one of the areas where little progress has been achieved to date. It is almost as if many bishops and priests still cling to what they perceive to be their exclusive "powers," and in some cases even feel threatened by this forward movement on the part of the laity. But where pastors and laity do work together as community, I have felt a special vibrancy and commitment to promoting the Reign of God through their words and actions.

One of the defining moments of Vatican II was brought into focus when Cardinal Josef Suenens made a proposal that had many bishops on the edge of their seats. He suggested it was time we took another look at what was happening. We were spending a lot of time and energy trying to understand better the nature of our Church, but there was a danger that we might spend too much time looking at ourselves while forgetting what our mission here on earth was all about. We appeared far too introverted and forgot that we had a mission to serve the world even more than to be concerned with our internal relationships. He suggested that we not only focus "within," but that we be equally concerned with what was happening to the rest of humankind, to the areas around us "without." Ultimately this shift brought about the longest of all the Council documents, *Gaudium et Spes* (The Church in the Modern World). It also gave rise to a new compassionate relationship with the world, with a renewed theology and language about God.

As I have lectured in many areas of the world, I have seen tears well up in the eyes of members of the audience after hearing these teachings of our Church. There arises a softness, a gentleness and an awe as they, along with me, attempt to digest the mystery of love that can overflow from a Christ-centred, biblical, loving and servant Church. Reflecting on the mystery of the human and the divine in history, I have heard people express forgiveness of themselves and their leaders, and have witnessed others ready to embrace a new maturity as pilgrim people.

The great liturgical renewal, which is one of the richest fruits of the Council, is centred on a basic understanding of worship as the work of Christ. The Paschal Mystery unfolds throughout the liturgical cycle, and the restoration of an understanding of Sunday as Sabbath reveals both its true meaning and dignity through this renewed understanding and appreciation.

Noteworthy as well is the instruction that pastors have a duty to ensure that all the faithful participate consciously, actively and fruitfully in the liturgy. When speaking to priests, I remind them that promoting lay participation should be a central concern in their ministry. Where holiness once appeared to be reserved to those church members who lived under religious vows or were ordained for official ministry, we have been reminded that all the faithful are called to that perfect holiness by which the Godhead is perfect in itself.

For succeeding generations, along with the present one, we felt it imperative to express our faith in terms that are understandable. The world is evolving, and while the message of Christ is always the same, how we experience it in our culture varies from place to place and from one era to the other. One constant was clear: faith comes through hearing and teaching. How will people hear if the preachers cannot communicate with them in meaningful language? The Word of God is alive and hence needs to be translated into contemporary terms to preserve its deeper intelligence and make manifest its meaning, precisely out of fidelity to its message. Likewise, the celebration of the Eucharist ought to be in a language that the people understand.

The significance of relating the Sunday (and daily) scripture readings to the signs of the times and to our daily lives can help heal the division between what we profess one day a week but are slow to enact on the other six. This rift is excoriated by Vatican II as one of the gravest dangers befalling our spiritual life, for it divorces belief from action. In the absence of God, every individual becomes a deity unto himself or herself and a society implodes spiritually. Understanding and participating in the liturgy can provide us with a constant infusion of spiritual nourishment that we can then begin to share with others.

Of course there were also documents from the Council on the Eucharistic sacrifice as source and summit of the Christian life, a saving activity in which we all have a part to play. The Eucharist can now be presented to believers as a verb rather than simply an object, as Jesus invited us to "do" this as he did: namely, to surrender ourselves in humble service, even at the cost of our lives, if need be. While our spiritual lives are centered on the Eucharist, I never heard a negative word about popular devotions at the Council: quite the opposite!

Vatican II also broadened our perception of what is known as the Real Presence. This refers to the sacred host, but it also includes the multiple other ways in which Christ is always present: in the person of the minister, in the sacraments and the Word, and in the total assembly's praying and singing. It is time that we move beyond a narrow and superficial theology that focuses on the tabernacle and host itself as if it were the only true presence of Christ.

I was very happy also to hear several Council Fathers, with support from our brother bishops from the Eastern churches, stress the role of the Holy Spirit in the celebration of the Eucharist. This led to the restoration of the "epiclesis" (invoking the Holy Spirit to "Bless and approve our offering") in the Canon of the Mass as well as the formulation of a series of new Canons where the focus is not on the special and particular words spoken by the celebrant, but on the telling of the sacred story by the president of the assembly.

It was my privilege to address the Council on four occasions and to submit a number of written documents, or *animadversiones*. One of my oral interventions addressed the twofold mission and role of the laity: lay people have as their mission the expression of their faith in the world arena as well as in the internal life of the Church. Another urged that we seek to overcome the unhealthy dichotomy between the spiritual and temporal realms. It has for too long been a custom to see them as opposites, as if there were two levels in creation, a higher and a lesser. My third address requested that the Council recognize the sacramental character of family life and particularly of conjugal intimacy. The fourth suggested that diocesan priests might develop their spirituality through the very exercise of their pastoral ministry, no less effectively than through a routine of monastic exercises.

In convening the second session of the Council, Pope Paul VI offered four points that could guide the Council. He called for an examination of the Church in itself, with emphasis on the role of the bishops as pastors. He looked forward to a complete renewal of the Church and to the promotion of Christian unity, with an accent on pardon and forgiveness. He also gave an extended description of what he called the "Dialogue of Salvation" *(Ecclesiam Suam)*, an important topic as we look to the future. Perhaps the best summary of all our deliberations, and a good formula for us today, is found in these words, from *Gaudium et Spes*: "Let there be unity in what is necessary, freedom in what is unsettled, and charity in any case."

Jesus told his disciples that after he had sent them the Holy Spirit, they would achieve "even greater things." As I travel and lecture, I encounter many people who find liberation in hearing those words. Some listeners in the audience even begin to ask, "Can I really accomplish 'even greater things'? How can the community of faith achieve that?" I have no answer to their queries, but remind them that they know the signs of the times in their own lives. To read those signs, and to act accordingly, is to begin to live out the mystery and the promise that the Second Vatican Council reminded us is both our heritage and our privilege in this world that we, for the moment, call home.

My main regret is that all this came to me almost like a belated acquisition rather than a childhood heritage. Still, I will be forever grateful to Blessed John XXIII for having accepted to be God's messenger at such a propitious time. And for me, what a blessing to have been chosen to serve as a Council Father! What a privilege for all of us to share in this providential surge in the life of our beloved Church!

4

"ADSUMUS": WE ARE HERE

"*Adsumus, Domine Sancte Spiritus, adsumus*" (We are here, Holy Spirit, we are here). These words opened every session of the Second Vatican Council as we prayed for guidance and inspiration, and for the ability to combine justice, love and faithfulness. It was impossible to have anticipated the breadth and depth of the process that Blessed John XXIII set in motion when he startled the entire world with his plan to convene an Ecumenical Council. What a surprise gift from heaven in the person of this creative Pope, who some expected would be merely an interim "caretaker"! There were many areas where Vatican II represented real progress in the appreciation and understanding of our Catholic faith. I personally underwent a profound conversion of heart and mind. What I offer here is but a partial list of the themes upon which I was called to reflect and pray. They may help readers to appreciate better the vast scope, creative insights and continuing relevance of Vatican II.

From a pastoral perspective, I have been most affected by the document called *Gaudium et Spes* (The Church in the Modern World). It includes so much rich material that it is difficult to summarize adequately. (I encourage people to read it, as well as the other documents, in their fullness.) It begins with a proclamation of the Church's solidarity with today's world, "the joys and hopes, the grief and anguish," especially of the poor and afflicted. It acknowledges not only that the Church is in history, but that history is also in the Church. It emphasizes the mystery of humanity made clear in the mystery of the Word made flesh, the model of the perfect human, and the possibility of reflecting the Holy Trinity through the gift of oneself through love. Reverence for every human person as another self follows, and must shape our social values.

Those values, however, are not necessarily the same in all societies. Some of the difficulties we faced stemmed from huge cultural differences; how the Church adapts to non-Christian cultures was one of the basic pastoral issues discussed at the Council. It is still apparent today that the Latin-European mentality is dominant in our Church. It pains me greatly to feel that Church leaders do not always comprehend the importance of inculturation. I sense there is sometimes even a tinge of racism in the highly centralized approach to proposed solutions to this problem. This conviction gradually arose in me as I experienced worship in areas such as India, Africa, Latin America and China. We are still far from a just, satisfactory and truly meaningful resolution, and these tensions are also implicit in ecumenical ventures, even when not openly discussed.

Gaudium et Spes makes clear that we as a Church are first and foremost intimately related to humankind as a whole. We are called not to condemn the world but to render service to it in the light of the Gospel values with which we seek to transform it. We share with compassion the hopes and anguish of society. We do not flee from, but instead welcome, the global changes that are occurring and to which we hope to make a spiritual contribution. Like other people, we, too, are wrestling with the fundamental deeper questions that lie in the hearts of human beings today, such as questions of meaning, survival, and the global redistribution of resources to ensure a basic minimum of well-being for every inhabitant of this planet.

All this seems an enormous expectation to place on one another. But we are not left to ourselves in our quest for social justice: the divine seed in humanity is capable of seeking and discerning signs of God's presence and purpose in the happenings, needs and desires of today. *Gaudium et Spes* reminds us that all are created in God's likeness and are no different from ourselves: "every type of discrimination … is to be overcome and eradicated as contrary to God's intent," and all of us have a sacred obligation to mould a new humanity.

We are all encouraged to shoulder our own responsibility in forming our conscience and not to hesitate to take the initiative as "citizens of the world." All too often, the initiatives do not come from our denominational institutions. It is painfully obvious to me that there is often a discrepancy between what we profess and how we lead our daily lives. (Chesterton wisely observed that "Christianity has not been tried and found wanting; it has been found difficult and not tried.") Translating faith into social issues is challenging and can be risky. It is easier to stand back and hope others do the work. Such aloofness will not convince the world that social justice is indeed a priority for members of the Church. Those who decide that their piety is best served by withdrawing from temporal affairs, who separate religion from daily life, are warned by the Council that this dichotomy constitutes a grievous error.

We do not have to look in unusual places: the ordinary circumstances of daily life provide us with countless opportunities to transform the world through love. With this ongoing call to transcendence, the goal of human perfection, remote as it may seem, becomes the new commandment of love.

The Church does in fact also learn from society. We can strive to discern the many voices of our times and interpret them in the light of God's word. Again, this is everybody's task – it is not just reserved for clergy in the pulpit, but is ready to be undertaken by all who wish to understand more clearly the operation of the Holy Spirit in the world today. Culture leads us to new understandings of humanity, and we are, I believe, witnessing the birth of a new global vision as we awaken more and more to our role in the cosmic evolution. With this comes the potential birth of a new humanism, one in which the human being is defined, according to *Gaudium et Spes*, first of all by responsibility towards one another and towards history. And while the Church seeks to enter into communion with various cultures, it is, ultimately, bound to none. A large challenge we face is to develop and maintain a strong harmony between Church and culture.

Other areas with which we as Council Fathers were concerned (and which were also confronted in *Gaudium et Spes)* were labour and leisure; principles for socio-economic life; ownership and private property as a condition for civil liberty; economics and Christ's Kingdom; and the work of justice under the inspiration of charity. We also entered new territory with notes on political life, the healing and liberating power of nonviolence, the arms race, the "savagery of war," and the role of the international community.

Peace was claimed to be the work of justice and the fruit of love, to be developed constantly in collaboration with all people of good will. In a section on "The Avoidance of War," *Gaudium et Spes* stated that, in attempting to foster peace within the community of nations, the Church maintains an "unequivocal and unhesitating condemnation" of war against defenseless people as a crime against both God and humanity. I was one of those who hoped for an outright condemnation of modern warfare. It no longer meets the moral criteria or conditions under which it might be accepted as a lesser evil and a legitimate form of defense. But the spectre of communism, which still hung over Europe in those days, proved to be too much, and a compromise stance was adopted as the only possibility at that time. Would that the world might have listened more attentively to what Pope John XXIII urged in his final encyclical, *Pacem in Terris* (Peace on Earth). Broadening the range of Catholic social teachings, he addressed, among other issues, the problems of war and peace, and called for negotiation over armaments and human rights for all. His teachings set the stage for Pope Paul VI's declaration to the United Nations in 1965: "No more war, war never again!" We Council Fathers also rejected war as a solution to world problems. Focusing particularly on the methodical extermination of entire groups of humans, we declared that these and similar actions against innocent victims must be vehemently condemned as horrendous crimes.

We recognized that there could not be any final or definitive word on these complex matters. It was understood that the Council's work would have to be further pursued and amplified, since it dealt with matters in a constant state of development and flux within individual nations. But Vatican II issued a strong plea to world leaders and opinion shapers in saying that the Church calls for dialogue, about which Pope Paul VI wrote eloquently in his 1964 encyclical, *Ecclesiam Suam* (On the Church).

The renewed commitment of the preferential option for the cause of the poor, which was later proclaimed by Latin American bishops, was already latent in *Gaudium et Spes*. Subsequently, in 1971, the Synod of Bishops in Rome made the practical application of Vatican II teachings to the local scene by stating firmly that "action on behalf of justice and participation in the transformation of the world fully appears to us as a constitutive dimension of the proclamation of the Gospel." The Good News is best preached when there is a visible and tangible response to situations of manifest injustice.

Not Just for Catholics

Ecumenism and interfaith developments saw the influence and power of friendship and its magnetic attraction manifest in leaders like Blessed John XXIII. Vatican II would never have witnessed the presence and effective participation of so many Observers, or caught the imagination of the worldwide media, had it not been for the amiability, charm and radiance of Good Pope John. It was by patiently listening to each other's pastoral experience, and charitably but frankly offering amendments where needed, that we began to see emerging what eventually proved to be a larger picture of the truth. Here was where teamwork proved so valuable, and where ecumenical understanding flourished. Theologians and historians of calibre helped us to return to our roots. Protestant and Anglican Observers shared their own special insights, and we all made progress in our search for truth. This could on occasion be a painful experience, but we also developed lasting friendships.

My own journey towards fuller ecumenical understanding moved swiftly during the Council. I had been brought up to shun any contact with Protestants in our village of Swan Lake. Meeting shining personalities such as Robert McAfee Brown and Dr. Albert C. Outler completely altered my perception, as I trust it also affected theirs. As a matter of fact, I have a copy of an address McAfee Brown made to a gathering of Canadian bishops in Rome right after the Council, in which he expressed his joyful amazement at what the Church had achieved by way of reform.

Acknowledging the faith heritage of Abraham and Sarah, and rejoicing in the Covenant, we also expressed our indebtedness to, and solidarity with, our Jewish brothers and sisters. We deplored all forms of hatred, persecution, discrimination and anti-Semitism. In the wake of Vatican II, we would now in fact say that these attitudes are not only "deplored" but also strongly "condemned."

Often, during the debates on religious freedom, I discerned a very valuable lesson about the differences between cultures. Many bishops from countries that had a Concordat with the Vatican still accepted the thesis that error had no rights and that truth could be enforced and error repressed by power. In areas where democracy was established, like North America, the distinction prevailed between error and persons who were perceived to be in error. We began to understand what it meant to find *Semina Verbi* (seeds of the Word) – a term that was initially applied to Mission lands – now appropriate everywhere. The Spirit of the Lord animates all of creation. We do not bring religion to non-Catholic or "pagan" lands, but rather we recognize that the Divine is at work throughout the universe and beyond the visible boundaries of the Church. In the central Mystery of the Word Incarnate, we appreciate the beauty and power of Truth wherever it is found. It is no longer a question of "we are right" and "everyone else is wrong," but of being partners in the search, with each of us sharing fully and generously the substance of what we have received through the Holy Spirit.

Another great scholar whom I came to know was Father John Courtney Murray, S.J. He deserves much credit for his contribution to the teachings found in *Dignitatis Humanae*, the declaration on

Religious Freedom. This brilliant thinker maintained that Catholicism was fully compatible with democracy. He was brought to Rome by Cardinal Spellman of New York and gradually acquired great influence; despite determined resistance from some quarters, his persuasion won the day. He argued that religion had been perceived all too often as coercing the "irreligious" instead of respecting their positions. Both Pope Pius XII and John XXIII had spoken earlier about the responsibility of pursuing truth and the required freedom from coercion that are a consequence of humans being made in the image of God. I try to read and reflect regularly on the teachings concerning the relationship of the People of God to those who have not yet heard or accepted the Gospel, but who faithfully follow the dictates of their conscience.

Matters Dear to My Heart

My understanding of a pastoral council is one that touches on the core issues affecting people's lives and offers them affirmation, inspiration, and opportunities to dialogue about matters of significance to them. I felt very strongly about a number of pastoral matters, including the role of women and the sacramental nature of marital intimacy.

I had prepared for the latter topic by calling a meeting of married people on Vancouver Island. I had asked them to discuss some specific issues affecting their lives as couples, and to indicate what they expected from the Council. The fact that lay people had participated in the formulation of my submission to the Council attracted the attention of the press.

My intervention on conjugal love helped underscore the idea of marriage not as a contract so much as a covenant, with marital intimacy at its core. Some considered it an important formulation of the significance of the "domestic church," which is served by conjugal love in marriage. A married couple and their children can in fact be compared to a small community united by life and love, serving not only the Church but also the whole of human society. Ultimately, the sacrament of marriage associates humans with the divine creative love, thereby enhancing their dignity. Thirty-three Canadian bishops appended their signatures to the intervention. The subject was also addressed by several other speakers. (The entire English text of my spoken intervention may be found in Appendix I at the end of this book.)

Another topic on which I presented two oral interventions was the role of the laity. This I approached from a twofold perspective. On October 7, 1964, I addressed the Council Assembly in the name of a group of fifteen Canadian bishops. Among other things, I stated that the apostolic commitment of the laity in the temporal sphere, which seeks the promotion of humanity and the transformation of the world, is not only a humanitarian endeavour. It touches the very heart of the divine redemptive plan. The specific apostolate of the laity *as laity,* strictly speaking, differs substantially from the apostolate of the hierarchy.

There is also but *one* vocation of the laity to the apostolate. But it has a twofold aspect that concerns both the natural and the supernatural levels. Every lay person is called to assume responsibility for the welfare of both the temporal and spiritual orders. Separated from the lay apostolate, the hierarchical apostolate alone could not effectively achieve the human and divine transformation of the universe. Lay people can and do enter spheres to which the hierarchy normally have no access. The laity can bring to visibility newer and untouched areas of science and technology, opening them to Gospel insights and values. Where we once spoke of the "hierarchical apostolate" as representing the entire Church, we are now graced with a deeper and fuller understanding of the basic baptismal vocation of all believers.

Here is what I submitted to the Council on October 26, 1964, as the conclusion of my spoken presentation:

Christians achieve their total vocation when in the spirit of Christ they engage themselves in the structures of the world, share in its struggles and commune with the inner dynamism of humanity. Indeed they fulfill the very mission of the Church herself ... No one can effectively collaborate in developing the Christian community unless they actively participate in building the human community. Here lies the deep and ultimate meaning of charity. For charity does not concern only a limited number of actions added on to our human vocation. Love must order the whole life of the Christian.

All believers – both clergy and lay – are called to the fullness of life and perfection of charity: the laity are specially called to transform the world, inspired by Gospel values, and the clergy are to encourage and support the laity in this vocation. Lay people are recognized as fully competent, and are sometimes obliged to express their opinions and offer their insights for the good of the Church. Even as I spoke, I could sense, almost palpably, the process of this concept's growth in the hearts and minds of the Council Fathers.

I also made a written presentation when the topic of missions was under discussion, arguing for a fuller role for women:

> Given the Church's tradition, particularly as it relates to dea-
> conesses, given the need for a balanced pastoral approach,
> given that we as Christians are all called to serve, given that
> we as church have not fully recognized the unique contribu-
> tion of women, we suggest that a theology of ministry acces-
> sible to women, accompanied by appropriate canonical law,
> be undertaken and elaborated. We find it necessary that this
> Council open doors for a deeper collaboration of women in
> the Church's apostolic mission.

In retrospect, one can perceive many limitations in the way the Council was organized and conducted. The process was cumbersome and much time was needlessly lost. Unilateral presentations without discussion is not the most fruitful way towards deeper knowledge. Certainly, the entire enterprise could have been enriched by greater participation on the part of lay women and lay men. One can humbly recognize that debilitating problems endured. Despite those short-comings, I am truly thankful that the Council reached a successful conclusion and remains to this day a beacon of light.

However intense the labours, the Council also made provision for some breaks or time off. Memorable among these was attending the Eucharistic Congress in India in 1964. Sitting beside me during the session that year was the auxiliary bishop of Bombay (now Mumbai),

India. Bishop William Gomes confided to me that he would be returning to India before the end of the current session because he was in charge of preparations for the impending Eucharistic Congress, during which Pope Paul VI would visit India.

I ventured to offer assistance in any way I could during my stay there. I knew that preparations for the event included the consecration of four churches. In fact, on the Friday night before the celebrations, while I was at a gathering of pilgrims in the convent of the Sacred Heart Sisters, I received an urgent telephone call from "Willie." A situation had developed whereby both he and the Ordinary, Cardinal Archbishop Valerian Gracias, were committed to meeting arriving dignitaries and were thereby unable to preside at the consecration of the Cathedral. Would I please step into the breach and take over? Counting on a previous experience when I had served as assistant master of ceremonies, I agreed to preside. I knew all the ministers would be waiting for instructions, so I took the stance of a sergeant major and guided them through the proceedings. I knew no one was experienced enough to find fault with anything we might do. Thanks to their willing collaboration, everything flowed smoothly. To this day, visitors may find my name inscribed in the beautifully decorated Register or guest book near the main entrance in the foyer of the Cathedral.

Catholic Action

Perhaps one of the most significant things to blossom at and after the Vatican Council was what is known as "Catholic Action." Catholic action means people: the outward reach of the Church into the hearts of humanity. It includes social justice and human rights, the developing nations and the marginalized poorest of the world, war and peace, nuclear weapons and the real nature of economics. I had read about this new development while I was studying at the Major Seminary. That was when I first learned the name of the renowned Belgian priest Canon Josef (Joseph) Cardijn. It was my privilege to meet him the following summer at an international convention in Montreal. I introduced myself to him in our common native tongue, Flemish. It was the beginning of a long and rewarding friendship.

In my earlier ministry, when I was named diocesan director of Catholic Action, I learned a tremendous amount from its dedicated young people, who, with their high ideals, strove to make the world a better place. They were quick to grasp how the gospel is to be proclaimed in ways amenable to the modern mind and attractive to the heart. I developed enduring friendships with several of these young people, who later became some of the movers and shakers whose leadership greatly benefits society and the world at large.

Catholic Action was first suggested by Pope Pius X as a formula whereby the laity could help the Church in the restoration and promotion of true Christian civilization under the direction of ecclesiastical authority. It was formally authorized or "mandated" by Popes Pius XI and Pius XII, and was described as the collaboration with, or participation in, the apostolate of the hierarchy. It was subject as well to the "mandate" of the local bishop. It developed a variety of forms and spread through many countries. Canon (later Cardinal) Cardijn promoted it very successfully among young workers. He provided it with its now classic formula: observe, judge, act.

This movement was one of several precursors to Vatican II, along with the liturgical renewal, updated religious education, and social reform movements. Gradually, more autonomous forms developed. Many of the Catholic Action groups began to wane when Vatican II proclaimed its teaching about the baptismal priesthood. Lay people became aware that their true calling was based on their baptism and confirmation. Therefore, this calling did not require the intervention of the hierarchy. It was now understood that the baptismal priesthood of the people contained in itself the mandate to proclaim the Gospel and live the Beatitudes. The Spirit imparts divine gifts freely, and believers need not wait to undertake their mission in life.

Later, at Vatican II, Cardinal Cardijn confided to me that he never fully succeeded in getting "those Romans" to grasp the true nature of specialized (meaning the apostolate of like to like) Catholic Action. They failed to grasp how it was directed primarily towards the transformation of society through Gospel values. It was not meant to be oriented towards the strengthening or promotion of Church structures as such. I remember him bemoaning the fact that in the commission in which he participated during the Council, he had found it practically impossible to get the members to understand the true nature of Catholic Action.

Huge Tasks Await

In some ways, it had been simpler to keep the Gospel separate from the messy issues of the day. I can still remember from my own training the dichotomy of "bad world – holy Church," which kept sacred things separate from the secular. This view was upheld by having a sacred language, Latin. Once it was accepted that the liturgy was to be celebrated in the vernacular, although in a very restricted way initially, the floodgates opened. Things quickly broadened beyond having just the Mass readings read in the people's own tongue. It meant that all cultures were now acceptable organs or agents for proclaiming the Good News. Latin lost the monopoly of "orthodoxy." We became aware that the Spirit works through any culture or language, and that no tongue has a particularly holy quality. This movement towards universality and a more global mentality is surely part of the "New Pentecost" that Pope John XXIII welcomed.

Something must be said here about the relationship of the Eucharist to the Church. Much remains to be done in both theory and practice. The movement forward has been agonizingly slow. I remember Father (later Cardinal) Yves Congar, O.P. speaking to our group of Canadian bishops; we had gathered to hear him share some Church history with respect to the Eucharist. He reminded us that in the first millennium, the Eucharist formed the Church: "where Eucharist is celebrated, there is the Church." During the second millennium, the Church, by then identified with the hierarchy, began to "make" the Eucharist. A variety of administrative regulations concerning "Real Presence" reduced it to only the visibility of the host, and the introduction of elevations. It was time now, he declared, to restore the balance.

The failure to respect the full ecclesial dimensions of these teachings is, I believe, responsible in good part for the failure to provide Eucharist wherever it is needed. Similarly, the resistance in the Latin

Rite to the ordination of experienced and qualified married men – *viri probati* – as has always been the norm in the Eastern Rites, such as the Ukrainian or Byzantine, is connected to this history.

Linked with all the above is the restoration of the cup to the Laity. The refusal of communion under both kinds was one of the major sources of conflict with Luther as expressed in the decisions of the Council of Trent. Vatican II also authorized the restoration of the permanent diaconate, inclusive of married men, which restored an ancient dimension of our Catholic beliefs, life and practice.

Lastly, the Council reaffirmed the principle of subsidiarity, which means that the central authority, the Vatican, should not perform functions that agents closer to the scene (dioceses) can fulfill. This tension between the periphery and the centre was a major issue throughout our deliberations, and is far from being resolved. Local synods with governing as well as consulting authority could be convened. But power does not readily surrender its power. The principle of subsidiarity and consultation inspired me, however. When I returned to Victoria, I held a series of consultations that culminated in a diocesan synod. The synod brought Vatican II home to our local church, and was one of the most exciting and concrete outcomes of the Council for our diocese.

Nobody, not even Pope John XXIII, expected that Vatican II would turn into such a vast enterprise or last as long as it did. Pope Paul VI did what he could to expedite matters, but there was simply too much work to be attended to, though we struggled along bravely. Towards the end, a form of psychological fatigue set in. I felt weary and apprehensive, yet exhilarated. We began to look forward to the Council finally drawing to a close. In reality, it had hardly begun.

We have huge pastoral tasks awaiting us. Global peace calls for the work of justice and will be the fruit of love, never of war. Dialogue, not competition, still less aggression, offers the true and sure path towards a civilization of love. As Teilhard de Chardin ventured to declare years ago, the future of humanity rests with people who can provide coming generations with reasons for living and for hope. He went on to encourage us by saying that, when we learn to "harness for God the energies of love," the world will once again have discovered fire.

PART TWO

EXPECTATIONS
IN VICTORIA

5

NEW BISHOP, OLD DIOCESE

Flying off to the Vatican Council in 1962, immediately after being named Bishop of Victoria, was a remarkable start to my episcopate! Yet despite the importance of the Council, I was instructed by the Pope's representative in Ottawa to proceed to Victoria and take possession of my diocese as soon as possible. Given that I still had to terminate many tasks in my Manitoba parish and be ordained in St. Boniface Cathedral before flying to the west coast, I left the first session of the Vatican Council before it ended.

There followed a hectic, and sometimes very emotional, time from late November well into December, as, with the help of my dedicated staff at Holy Cross, we put everything in order, preparing for my ordination as bishop and my departure. To give the bishops returning from the Council time to travel to Saint Boniface, the date for the ceremony was set for December 14, 1962.

The Cathedral was packed for the ordination. A mixture of emotions and thoughts welled up in my heart and mind as I knelt before the presiding bishops, of whom Archbishop Maurice Baudoux was the principal celebrant.

I was greatly reassured by the company of many friends praying with me and wishing me well. There was also a painful tearing at my heart as I felt myself being pulled away from those same cherished friends and the familiar parochial environment that I had come to love dearly. Apprehension hung over me like a menacing cloud as I prepared to venture into an unknown and as yet mysterious new world. Through it all came the remembrance that a calling to divine service always brings with it the strength of the Holy Spirit and the graces to discern my future paths as a pilgrim progressing in the Reign of God. I somehow sensed in my inner being that all would be well.

On December 19, a party of relatives and friends accompanied me on the flight to Vancouver. Upon landing we were met by a group that included the Coadjutor Archbishop Martin Johnson. He informed me that Archbishop William Duke, who was to preside over my installation, had been taken seriously ill and would not be present. Archbishop Johnson offered to accompany me to the hospital for a brief courtesy call. From his bed, Archbishop Duke greeted me warmly. He wished me well, assured me of his prayers and asked for my blessing. I in turn asked for and received his blessing. I said goodbye to him with the premonition that I would never see him again.

The next day my family group and I boarded the *Queen of Victoria* ferry, bound for Vancouver Island. We arrived in mid-afternoon. My first courtesy call was at Government House. His Honour the Lieutenant Governor George R. Pearkes, V.C., gave me a very gracious reception and a cordial welcome to British Columbia. He also attended the installation ceremony at St. Andrew's Cathedral later that evening. Then I was driven to my new home at 740 View Street. A large and joyful crowd had assembled in front of the bishop's residence, including 33 priests from the diocese, who later gave their pledge of obedience to their new leader; a number of Sisters of St. Ann, with a whole group of students; plus many other well-wishers. I was tremendously heartened by the warm welcome. As well, I was encouraged by the many expressions of affection and promises of support with which the people of Vancouver Island showered me.

Upon entering the residence, I was introduced to the diocesan priest Consultors, to whom I presented my credentials. That involved showing them the Vatican document known as a "Bull" – a large parchment signed by Pope John XXIII attesting to the fact that he had designated me Bishop of Victoria. It was now time for my formal installation. After vesting, we moved in procession from the residence into the Cathedral. I had never been there before and felt a sense of apprehension as the full weight of my new responsibilities settled upon my shoulders. What an awesome task to accept the leadership of all these people who filled every available space in the Cathedral!

There was an impressive group of special guests, including representatives of provincial and local government as well as of other Christian churches. In my first address, I thanked all the participants for their hearty welcome. I expressed the hope that there would be continued collaboration between the State and the Church. I also expressed my conviction that "Man without God is not fully human." These words were meant to be an indication of the orientation I intended to follow in my task as bishop. I also remember a sense of elation as I helped distribute the Eucharist to the seemingly endless lines of people who presented themselves for Communion. What had for some time appeared to me as a kind of dream now became reality. I was ministering to my new family of believers.

One of the most important things to come out of Vatican II was the spirit of cooperation and shared ministry for priests and laity. I wanted to implement this approach at the very start of my work in my new diocese. My first consultation was with the diocesan priests. We held our first working and pastoral review, and I assured them that I would be counting very much on their advice. I also outlined some of my initial plans. I was anxious to share the orientations I had gathered from the first session of the Vatican Council. They listened respectfully, but I did not initially perceive any great enthusiasm on their part. I assured myself that this was quite understandable, partly because, with one exception, they were all older than I. At that moment I really did feel like the "Benjamin Bishop."

This island was my new diocese, and was to be my home for many years. Compared to the harsh winters in Manitoba, I was in a paradise of warmth, lush vegetation, fishing and forest resources, and people with varied cultural and religious backgrounds. I was soon to learn what lay ahead for me on this most western island of Canada: the challenges of being on an island included a widespread and limited number of Catholics and of resources available to the faithful. I was in a diocese that had been established in 1846, with a rich history and established customs, and I was only 38. What would my life as a young man and bishop be in this place?

I began to make the rounds of the diocese, spending at least a full day with each parish priest, who in turn introduced me to people in the local community. As I moved about the Island, I was warmly received despite my being a complete stranger and appearing to be so young that some jokingly referred to me as the "boy bishop." I surprised people by promptly acquiring my own car instead of being chauffeured around, as was the custom of the time.

The media were very sympathetic and I received many requests for interviews, as well as invitations to address a variety of groups. The mood of the time also encouraged me to develop my ecumenical con-tacts, a dimension of episcopal ministry that I have found very inspiring and uplifting. The veteran Anglican Archbishop Harold Sexton was especially friendly and effectively assisted me as a mentor on a number of occasions. Later on, in 1968, he would proudly present me to the worldwide Anglican Episcopate gathered at the Lambeth Conference. It was the first time in history that the Vatican had sent Observers to this event, and I was honoured to be one of the seven. I also enjoyed a lengthy conversation with Her Majesty Queen Elizabeth II on that occasion, and realized why she is known as possibly the best-informed woman in the world.

Besides meeting people and forming working relationships, I was also very interested in knowing more about the island that was now my home. While doing some research in the very modest dioc-esan archives, I learned some of the long and fascinating history of Vancouver Island, the land of many First Nations peoples. One of the most heart-warming encounters I had with them was a special event sponsored by several tribes that live in this territory. It took place on February 14, 1963, and was held in the huge longhouse in the Tsawout East Saanich Indian Reserve near Sidney. It began with a ceremonial canoe ride, recalling the arrival of the first bishop, Msgr. Modeste Demers. After the welcome by one of the leaders, I was invited to plant a large wooden cross fashioned from a cedar tree. We then processed to the longhouse, where a large, crackling fire had been lit at both ends of the building. Chiefs from several tribes made speeches marking their accord with the purpose of the ceremony. I, in turn, presented a ceremonial woollen blanket to each orator. Then two elderly women approached and placed a decorated blanket on my shoulders. "Now you are one of us, you belong to us," was the theme of the comments made by several of the Chiefs. I was given my new name, "Siem Le Pleet S'HWUWQUN," which translates as "Great High Priest White Swan," indicating that I was now formally adopted into the Indian race. It was with great satisfaction that the attendants learned I had been born in the village of Swan Lake, Manitoba. Ever since then, I have been greeted as a Native Elder when I visit a reserve or meet a group of First Nations people.

A New Coat

Shortly after my appointment as Bishop of Victoria, I was advised that it was customary for bishops to have a coat of arms. A friend directed me to a businessman in New York, Bill Ryan, whose hobby was genealogy heraldry. On my way back from Rome at the end of the first session of Vatican II, I visited Bill. He showed me his library, which featured an array of family genealogy dictionaries. To my delight I learned that both sides of my family, the De Papes and the De Roos, had coats of arms. We had recourse to them as we fashioned my personal coat of arms and in elaborating a coat of arms for the diocese, which previously had not had one.

The De Pape's insignia had three towers and a chevron stripe. Pope John XXIII's coat of arms had one tower, and since "Pape" means "Pope" in English, I inserted a tower into mine to honour them both.

My father's crest had three falcons and a chevron stripe, so I inserted a falcon for him. The chevron stripe I kept as common to both families. My original personal contribution is a "shell" distributing three drops of water, symbolizing baptism in the name of the Blessed Trinity. This links me to my patron, Saint Remi, Archbishop of Reims in France, who baptized Clovis, King of the Francs. The original family shields had a field of blue, which I changed to red, colour of charity, to match my personal motto, taken from Ephesians 4.16: "to build in love" (*aedificatio in caritate*).

Having learned the principles of the elements of coats of arms, I also designed one for the diocese, since there was none at the time of my arrival. Its design includes a wavy line signifying water (encircling the whole, it represents an island). Superimposed on this is the cross of St. Andrew, with a stylized crown recalling Queen Victoria. An informed person will read: "St Andrew's at Victoria, on the Island."

When a bishop is in office, the two coats are joined together. As a retired bishop, should I choose to make a private copy, my own crest would occupy the entire shield.

My Native Brothers and Sisters

On New Year's Day every year, the Lieutenant Governor held a public reception; it was on that occasion that I learned of the British custom whereby a local church leader could commandeer a ship to transport him in case of need to any location where his presence was required. In this way I found myself on board HMCS *Beacon Hill*, a frigate, on June 3, 1963. While observing naval manoeuvres and chatting with the captain, I learned by telegram that Pope John XXIII had died. Later that day, the ship lowered a small boat (known as a piping) to deposit me at Tofino. The entire population of the village had turned out to watch the unusual performance, which was how they caught their first glimpse of the new bishop. I spent that night across the bay at the Indian Residential School. The next day, I presided at a solemn pontifical Requiem High Mass, with the entire school participating, in memory of our beloved Pope. I can still hear the note of deep sorrow in a Protestant minister friend's voice as he addressed me, with tear-filled eyes, after the death of Good Pope John. Not only did he offer me his condolences, but he declared, in the spirit of true ecumenism, "We have lost our Pope." Naturally, the friendly spirit of Blessed John XXIII had exerted its own special charisma and charmed everyone, whether they were affiliated with the Catholic Church or not.

During that same month, Father Art Leonard guided me through an extensive tour of all the Native reserves. Each place held welcoming dances and hosting ceremonies and referred to my status as an adopted brother. This gave me an early introduction into the fine qualities of our Native brothers and sisters and served to dispel completely the negative and racially biased impressions I had inherited as a child in Manitoba. I eventually worked with First Nations peoples on human rights and social justice issues, particularly as chairman of the British Columbia Human Rights Commission from 1973 to 1977. My heart is filled with gratitude for the many friendships I developed with a number of Native people during my years as bishop of Vancouver Island. Even in retirement, these friends welcome me at special events and recall my given name and my status as part of their family.

Of course I was not the only cleric to have a place in First Nations society. In 1977, I was approached by an Oblate Brother, Terrance McNamara, who had gained a high level of respect and affection among the First Nations people living in the southern part of Vancouver Island. He informed me that he felt called to the ordained ministerial priesthood and hoped to work with Native groups on the Island. However, his cultural commitments prevented his receiving seminary training during the winter dancing season. I was in favour of an experimental approach in the context of Aboriginal life, following the insights of Vatican II in matters of inculturation. I proposed an alternative program that would allow Terry to meet the expectations flowing from his adoption into the Indian race while getting the pastoral training commonly provided through residence in a seminary; his superiors also took into account his previous academic and pastoral experience. He was subjected to the usual rigorous scrutiny in order to qualify for admission to the Catholic priesthood. I offered to preside at his ordination with the understanding that he would continue to be a member of the Oblate community.

The ordination took place on July 15, 1979, in the Quamichan longhouse on Tzouhalem Road in Duncan, B.C., amid Indian ceremonies. We followed a process enriched by Native cultural expressions, which was greeted with enthusiasm by the Native people who attended and participated fully in this event. I wore a chasuble of buckskin adorned with native artifacts and colorful beadwork, which had been loaned for the occasion by Bishop Fergus O'Grady of Prince George. Later I appointed Terry episcopal vicar for the Native Peoples and Rector of Saint Andrew's Cathedral. Under his direction, an admirable new main altar and ambo, based on biblical themes matching the liturgical season, were designed by Native carver Charles Elliott. It was my hope that, as a result, Native people would feel more at home in the mother church of the diocese.

Land, Laity and Learning

There were, of course, a number of other matters that needed my attention, and I had to work with what was already in place even as I tried to incorporate the many new insights of the Council. My predecessor, Bishop James Michael Hill, was known for his caution as administrator. He had lived through the experience of the Depression and ran the diocese on a very small budget, smaller than the yearly budget of my former parish of Holy Cross in St, Boniface. Nor did Bishop Hill have a full-time staff; he had only a part-time secretary.

I learned that the only contribution the parishes were called upon to make to diocesan finances was a yearly collection. According to Church law, a diocesan bishop in Canada holds administrative office as a "Corporation Sole." He is responsible not only for the spiritual well-being of the diocese, but also for its financial security and stability, two major responsibilities. It was clear to me that very little new development of churches, schools and support programs for faith development would be possible without a secure financial system in place.

In consultation with local realtor Cy Montague, my Priest Consultors and a few other knowledgeable people, we began planning an ambitious project of increasing the land holdings of the diocese. Cy helped me obtain excellent sites at very good prices. Real estate was still very cheap and inflation was not yet the menace it would become later. Land was selling for as little as $5,000 per acre. The future looked encouraging and we anticipated the construction of new churches and schools in several locations. I eventually persuaded the parish leaders to accept a yearly diocesan tax based on an agreed percentage of their regular income. We formed a team for administration and began to formulate some mutually agreed upon policies for more effective and forward-looking development.

Imbued with Vatican II insights, I did my utmost to help the people to whom I ministered free themselves from the limitations that stifled much of their spirit of initiative. I was firmly convinced that baptized believers could be trusted to respond to the gifts imparted to all the faithful by the Holy Spirit. But not every member of the clergy was of that same mind. I had been advised by Father Paul Purta, a young and very spiritual retreat director who was sent to us in the summer of 1963 by the Sulpician Fathers from Washington State to direct the annual priests' retreat. I had deliberately requested that he listen very carefully to the priests during the spiritual exercises and give me his frank impressions of where I stood in this regard. I will never forget his observation: "They will respect you because of your Office, but do not expect them to understand you." Much as I sought to merit their confidence, keeping an open-door policy and listening as compassionately as I could to both their concerns and their suggestions, I sensed in a number of them a passive-aggressive attitude that I regretted but failed to overcome. I believe that an issue of "threatened power" underlies much of this attitude and may explain somewhat the lasting resistance to change. Not unlike all human institutions, a number of people caught the vision of Vatican II while others, fearing the changes might be more than they could tolerate, struggled to maintain the status quo.

While my ideal was, and is, that as we discern the movements of the Holy Spirit, we will respond with the "obedience of faith" recommended to us by the Scriptures, I would not allow negative resistance to mask my vision for the diocese. Trusting in the inspiration of the Vatican Council, I began to introduce consultative procedures with a view to developing anew a spirit of working together, both among the clergy and between priests and their parishes.

To encourage the priests of the diocese to participate more effectively in its governance, I established a Priests' Senate, which was elected by the clergy of the entire diocese. To further broaden the diocesan leadership, I also set up a Bishops' Council, later renamed the Diocesan Pastoral Council. I held regular meetings with both organizations. We designated a chairperson to guide us through our agendas, a process that made it easier to distinguish between my participation in the decision-making process during the discussions and my own subsequent decision-taking responsibilities as head of the diocese.

To encourage the laity, all the parishes of the diocese were invited to set up a parish council to share responsibility with their pastors. Their task would be to enhance the spiritual life of the parish, provide more effective organization, and promote greater participation of all the parishioners in parish life and in outreach to society at large. The priests themselves were reminded that their leadership role is one of service, not of domination. They were urged not only to consult parishioners on occasion, but also to invite them to help formulate policy and share in decision making.

To deepen the prayer life of the people, we also started a Prayer Companions movement. This was headed by a gifted and recently trained lay couple, Jim and Joan Felling. Candidates of all ages were invited to deepen their prayer life. They were familiarized with methods of prayer through a series of retreats and were initiated into the ways of mysticism. They eventually became qualified to facilitate retreats and perform the equivalent duties of spiritual directors. They were called Prayer Companions to make it clear that the Holy Spirit is the ultimate spiritual director and that we simply accompany one another without claiming special authority over other people's lives. I was delighted to see how the Holy Spirit can bestow upon people gifts that bring forth such rich and mature spiritual fruits.

Following the ecumenical example of Blessed John XXIII, I sought to work with other Christian churches as well. Having been informed that the University of Victoria was about to be established, Archbishop Harold Sexton and I submitted a proposal for an ecumenical college on campus. That proposal never came to fruition, but a few years later, Anglican Bishop Frederick Roy Gartrell and Rev. Albert E. King of the Metropolitan United Church joined me in establishing an ecumenical chaplaincy at the University of Victoria. In 1972, Father Leo Robert provided free and much-appreciated pastoral services to students on campus. He was joined the following year by Anglican priest Marlowe Anderson, and then by Clare Holmes of the United Church. They agreed to work together as an ecumenical team at the service of everyone on campus. The University of Victoria had initially described itself as resolutely "secular" and was not favourable to any formal religious presence on campus. However, the then President of the University had shared with me his desire to provide on campus what he called "spiritual values." I saw this as an opportunity to enrich the university campus with the Gospel message presented in an ecumenical form and context. From this was born the project of having a priest available to meet the spiritual needs of students and staff.

This new chaplaincy was received with such enthusiasm that representatives of several other faiths asked to join. Thus it grew into a substantial interfaith group. Today, women may equally serve as chaplains. The chaplaincy offers individual counselling, retreats, seminars on prayer, marriage preparation and forums on contemporary topics affecting the spiritual well-being of students, faculty and staff. Following the untimely death of Father Leo Robert in 1990, I appointed Sister Judy Morin, S.S.A., to replace him on the team. I understand that it is still flourishing and is making a great impact on the university.

I felt it was essential that our diocese be in tune with the renewed social teachings of Vatican II, which urged "action on behalf of justice" as well as the principle of freedom of speech. Diocesan leaders agreed with me in encouraging members of our faith community to engage in several areas, such as Development and Peace, the ecumenical development education Lenten program, prison ministry, Project North, and L'Arche, a movement of living with and for people with disabilities that had been founded by Jean Vanier. There was also renewed energy in St. Vincent de Paul, the Catholic Women's League, the Knights of Columbus, Basic Christian Communities, the Cursillo movement, the Housing Society in our Cathedral parish, the Provincial Council for Family and Children's Services, and charismatic prayer groups. The *Island Catholic News* was founded and served as a vehicle to educate people about the Council. We also set up a diocesan Social Justice office and a very effective Marriage Encounter team.

It may surprise some to know that, concerning the application or living out of Vatican II, I found that the most tangible appreciation for my leadership and the most effective support for my efforts came from the women religious of the diocese, a minority of exceptionally loyal lay leaders, and a few enthusiastic priests. The Women's Committee produced "A Plan for Study, Action and Growth," and a permanent Women's Commission later took over their work. One of the tools this group used was a national questionnaire entitled "Women in the Catholic Church," which was distributed throughout the diocese. More than 7,500 women from fifteen Western dioceses took part in this nationwide project, which helped me better grasp the issues affecting our diocese as well as the Church across Canada. I met frequently with its participants in our diocese, offered advice or made suggestions when requested, and presided at the Eucharist whenever I could. I was inspired by these contacts and greatly encouraged by the example of these dedicated and competent women.

Several Sisters of Saint Ann spearheaded a diocesan Office of Religious Education for developing educational policy, training catechists, helping parents in their role as faith models and teachers of their own children, and assisting parishes with their own local programs. One of the women shared with me her experience as a mother of four young children. She was very disappointed when she realized that there would be no priest or religious sister available to teach her children their catechism, so she took the training and proceeded to initiate them into their faith herself. "Now," she once declared to me, "if you sent someone to teach my children religion, I would not let you!" She had discovered and now joyfully claimed her own vocation to spiritual motherhood.

After the fourth and final session of the Council ended in 1965, I began a series of consultations with the faith community in our own local diocesan church. Many of the ideas that came out of the Council were new, unsettling or needed further elucidation. I visited all the parishes; during these parish visits, I enjoyed volunteering to assume the position of "bishop on the hot seat." I would invite people to raise with me any questions that preoccupied them. People generally responded with enthusiasm, and I in turn learned a lot in the process. The students at the University of Victoria are a good example of how this process worked. I found them very sincere, and together we discussed many significant issues of concern to them. The question that moved me most profoundly was the issue of faith: "Is it possible to continue to believe, in today's world?" This type of question was but one of many serious issues that bubbled up.

Historically, this was a well-established diocese. Its people were eager to mature in their faith. I frequently reflected on the Gospel image of "new wine in old wineskins," and on the rightness of "to everything there is a season," the admonition to "be not afraid," and my own motto, "to build in love." I fell in love with the people of Vancouver Island, marvelled at the island's beauty, and I decided I never wanted to leave it. My hopes were fulfilled and I continue to enjoy life here in retirement.

6

BEYOND VANCOUVER ISLAND

Pope John XXIII is reputed to have said, "I want to throw open the windows of the Church so that we can see out and the people can see in." Vatican II also opened the doors to allow the Holy Spirit in. The excitement over the Council's teachings generated new insights and energy in local parishes once people began to understand some of the implications. Many of the documents contained actions that could be implemented rather clearly, but others, as already noted, posed a problem for some of the faithful.

The use of the vernacular was one such problem. The principle had been formulated – that the use of the mother tongue could be extended beyond the scriptural readings during the Eucharist to other parts of the liturgy and sacraments, as determined by local bishops. However, the consequences went well beyond this cautious opening. It was as if a dam had burst and the vernacular just took over. Many lauded this initiative, while others regretted its introduction.

When I returned to Vancouver Island after the exhilarating experience of the Council, my work rapidly branched into two streams: one involved my experiences on Vancouver Island itself; the other was national and international. Sometimes they overlapped. Participants in the Council, particularly active Council Fathers, were much in demand as speakers, provided they were willing to endure the grinding regime of constant travel and public appearances. I became one of those itinerants, criss-crossing North America from Arizona to Alaska and from Victoria to St. John's. In reviewing the piles of documents and lecture notes that I have accumulated over 50 years, I have chosen to focus on those themes that gradually asserted themselves under unforeseen circumstances.

An almost endless list emerged: biblical spirituality, baptismal priesthood, religious education, human rights, women and the institutional Church, a theology of the Holy Spirit, adult maturity and progress in prayer, environmental concerns, the role of human beings in the cosmos, the interplay of religion and economics, "Free Trade" and global disparities, a pedagogy for social transformation, solidarity and Aboriginal rights, the role of Catholic hospitals, ecumenism and interchurch relations, faith in action and social justice, the preferential option for the poor, science and religion in dialogue, biblical characters and the Enneagram, peace, nuclear weapons and morality, the nature and exercise of authority, work and humanization, the political role of the Church, the cost of development, ecclesial developments in Latin America, China and Africa – the list of things dear to me seemed to expand indefinitely.

Looking back on all that transpired, I wanted to try to put it into a meaningful record and preserve some of my many experiences. With this in mind, I decided to review the limited number of personal files that I carried with me into retirement. Other files reside in the archives of the Diocese of Victoria, and the public files related to the Vatican Council are presently in the custody of the University of Victoria, in the Archbishop Seghers Collection. They were placed there with an imposing quantity of valuable ancient books that were in need of a special environment, as they are practically irreplaceable. (Thanks to the electronic age and digital research, the Collection can be browsed online via the University's Special Collections site.)

To my amazement, my searching turned up over 30 titles related to spheres of concern where I invested substantial amounts of energy during the over 37 years I served as Ordinary of the Victoria Diocese. Where to begin sorting all this history became something of a headache. Those who know me well will not be surprised that I decided to start with the subject of social justice. Hence, I will use that as my focus in recalling briefly what my ministry has been about throughout the greater part of my life.

Locally, social justice often dealt with Aboriginal civil rights. I have already described my initial encounters with the Native people on Vancouver Island, and how one of the first experiences I was graced with after my arrival was my adoption into the Native race. The friendships with which I was honoured there completely changed my understanding of and attitude towards my Native sisters and brothers.

On the National Stage

One of the most memorable situations where I was called upon to provide support to and solidarity with First Nations people dealt with energy development and the arena of reconciliation. The Berger Commission (also known as the Mackenzie Valley Pipeline Inquiry), led by Judge Thomas Berger, held part of its hearings near Fort Simpson in the mid-1970s. Local Aboriginals were concerned that building an oil pipeline might pose a threat both to the environment and to their land claims. I attended as a member of an ecumenical support group representing a coalition of mainline Christian churches, including the Canadian Conference of Catholic Bishops (CCCB).

On that occasion, I was asked to preside at a eucharistic celebration on a Sunday morning. I agreed on condition that the Native drummers who were available would take an active part. Unknown to me, this required some delicate negotiations with the local Chiefs, but the request was granted. A Native women's choir was assembled; they sang the entire Mass in Latin, as was still the custom in those days. An Anglican deacon accepted my invitation to proclaim the Gospel, thus highlighting the ecumenical dimension of our celebration. At the close of the Eucharist, I was graced with one of the most moving experiences I have ever known. As I was removing my vestments, the entire congregation surged forward, literally surrounding me and enveloping me with their broad smiles of appreciation and softly voiced words of thanks. I had the feeling that they were in their own way recognizing me as a spiritual leader and voicing their gratitude for the service I had rendered them by providing an opportunity for them to express their eucharistic thanksgiving on this important occasion in their lives. At the same time, I was saddened to ascertain that the local bishop had not seen fit to give priority to this event on his calendar. This denied a substantial part of his flock an opportunity to strengthen their bonds with the head of their local church, ordained to be the symbol and agent of their unity in faith.

Debate about the proposed pipeline occasioned the most intense day-long cross-examination I have ever endured. On April 18, 1977, I appeared before the National Energy Board in Ottawa, together with a team of four colleagues and representatives of other coalition members. Among other things, as mentioned earlier, we were calling for a moratorium on the building of the proposed Mackenzie Valley pipeline in the north.

We had submitted a brief in which our Social Affairs Commission stated in the name of the Roman Catholic bishops of Canada that as a people and a nation, we needed to take time to deal with some disturbing questions. These pertained to the setting of energy policy for the future and the impact of proposed developments on the lives and future of the Native peoples of Canada, as well as others in the north and south of the country. Under current circumstances, they were at the mercy of corporate decisions made without adequate and informed input from them.

Typical of the prevailing atmosphere at that time was the impassioned confrontation I endured from Mr. Pierre Genest, a lawyer for Canadian Arctic Gas Pipelines Ltd. Our lengthy exchange focused on the question of how we arrived at our moral or ethical judgments and whether these changed as facts evolved. The positive side was that this conversation provided an opportunity for our team to expound the basic Gospel principles on which we should be building our future, as well as the moral values pertinent to these and similar situations. Principles endure, but their application to specific issues may require a reinterpretation to remain understandable as cultures evolve and even the meaning of certain terms changes.

The Berger Commission decided to recommend a moratorium on the development of the Mackenzie Valley Pipeline. I was heartened that the Canadian bishops played a key role in this outcome.

Human Rights Affairs

Lack of attention to Native affairs was (and still is) a feature of civil life as well. Under Premier Dave Barrett, I was appointed as the first Chairperson of the newly established B.C. Human Rights Commission (1973–77). It was there that I witnessed clearly how Native people still have an uphill struggle with our justice system. Bridget Moran, in her book *Judgement at Stoney Creek*, relates the case of Coreen Thomas, a pregnant Carrier Native woman killed on Highway 16 in the early hours of July 2, 1976, by a car driven by Richard Redekop. The other Commission members agreed with me that we should attend the court hearings to draw attention to the deeper significance of how the process unfolded. In my opinion, it is still a moot point as to whether justice was served when, in June 1977, the accused was acquitted.

When I accepted to serve on the Human Rights Commission, I explained my decision at a gathering of the clergy. I claimed that as both a bishop and a citizen, it was my responsibility to render public service whenever possible. And what was more appropriate than for a Catholic bishop to help promote the cause of justice and human rights? I firmly believe that this is one area that requires action even more than verbal proclamations. I verified that not a single member of that group of clergy opposed my participation. Then I further informed them that out of respect for the varied backgrounds and sensitivities of the people my fellow members and I would be dealing with, I would not wear clerical dress when performing my civic duties. My experience since then has confirmed that this decision was indeed appropriate. Nor have I ever had to deal with any problems relating to my identity.

On the other hand, when I was once approached by a delegation requesting me to run for election and eventually serve in a political office, I made it clear that the responsibilities flowing from my ordination to ministerial office in the service of the Reign of God took priority over partisan politics, and that I was definitely not available.

Another human rights issue at the time was society's attitudes towards women, and the Church was not immune from such concerns. The United Nations declared 1975 to be International Women's Year; in preparation, the CCCB had issued a public statement that looked at ways of promoting awareness and understanding on issues of concern to women. I invited the women of our diocese to launch a program of their own. They began with a questionnaire that explored their attitudes towards the Church. I watched the process unfold from 1975 to 1983. At the time, Vancouver Island's Women's Committee, which was formed to guide their work, published "A Plan for Study, Growth and Action," which they addressed to the Western Conference of Catholic Bishops. Their study impressed me profoundly and I welcomed it wholeheartedly. It indicated "a tremendous need for the education of women, first of all to the Gospel, in the light of post-Vatican II theology and scholarship; secondly, to the need of developing or supporting women's own sense of self-worth; and thirdly, to raise women's awareness of the world beyond the parish and its needs." They made their own the Jungian notion that one's life task is to achieve harmony between the sexes, and to attain wholeness by integrating our subconscious component into the consciousness by relating to it, knowing it and incorporating it.

The Women's Committee welcomed the increasing signs of the emergence of women in the diocese. These women also recognized that the issue of whether women might be ordained to the ministerial priesthood was not the central issue. Rather, what was of primary importance was bringing about a more profound attitudinal change whereby the people, the hierarchy and the structures of the Church would accept women and men as having equal worth, dignity and responsibility, with their gifts of creativity, intuition, compassion and justice, which are so desperately needed. It was a great source of satisfaction for me to see these developments occurring.

The Bishops and the Economy

Other issues were also of major significance. One that generated an unforeseen magnitude of press coverage was the involvement of bishops in expressing their views on the Canadian economy. On New Year's Day in 1983, the CCCB's Social Affairs Commission, of which I was co-chair, published a declaration entitled "Ethical Reflections on the Economic Crisis." It was a time of social upheaval, with the Canadian government under pressure to bring meaningful solutions to problems that were frequently attributed to inflation. The bishops had watched these developments closely and were convinced that unemployment rather than inflation was the main culprit.

In 1980, Pope John Paul II had published *Laborem Exercens* (Through the practice of work), a magnificent encyclical on the topic of work. Among many other reflections, he elaborated on the nature of work as a humanizing factor. This deeper and broader philosophical and ethical study stood in sharp contrast with popular notions of work as "something you do to make money so you don't have to work." Our statement applied similar principles to the Canadian scene. Our view was that human beings are co-creators with God. Jesus once declared, "My Father is always working and I too am still working" (John 5.17). Vatican II also sees our liturgy itself as divine work.

"Ethical Reflections on the Economic Crisis" unleashed a storm of publicity. It held front-page attention for several weeks, and set the tone for other declarations. Many people came to consider the Catholic bishops as the "conscience of Canada." Tony Clarke, outstanding Director of Social Policy, together with the rest of the valiant staff of the CCCB Social Affairs Office, were overwhelmed with work. Bishop Adolphe Proulx, co-chair of the Social Affairs Commission, and I were in constant demand for conferences on this topic and related issues.

Our declaration was reported on around the world and was eventually translated into many languages. Its emphasis was on the vital ethical dimensions of economic discourse; the priority of people over material things; the dignity of working people, made in the image of God and called to be 'co-creators,' and hence the inherent dignity and immeasurable value of human work; and the priority of labour over capital and technology, not its "commodification." Due to the universal purpose of created things, there is a "social mortgage" on private property and on the means of production, because every human being has a right to the basic necessities and a decent income, and no one citizen has an absolute claim on natural resources. It follows that the needs of the poor must have priority over the wants of the rich. This must lead to a society based on compassion and justice rather than competition, and calls for authentic and lasting structural change.

This notion of change eventually required further attention. The members of the Social Affairs Commission turned their attention to the process whereby change takes place. We gradually developed a "methodology" for social change. To begin, we are called to establish contact with marginalized people and offer them our solidarity. Together we would verify the reality of their situation and engage in social analysis in the light of Gospel principles. We would then be in a position to support the poor, the marginalized and the oppressed in their cause, as they discern the appropriate methods for responding. Our role would be to help them develop their latent power, working in solidarity with them as they discover their own creativity. A compilation of the results, whether positive or negative, then brings about an assessment or evaluation, which helps to launch the next phase.

The entire process may be compared to a spiral rising and opening up to new movement. The 1971 Synod of Bishops in Rome declared that action on behalf of justice was a constitutive dimension of the proclamation of the Gospel. This represents, in my view, a practical application of what came to be known after Vatican II as the "preferential option for the poor." This new type of social engagement was first developed in Latin America as part of liberation theology. Liberation theology is not a subversive ideology, as some uninformed people have claimed, but a living force, inspired by the Bible, which shows us that God brings about salvation with and through the poor. The history of salvation is not written by the powerful and the rich, but rather by the helpless who put their trust in divine assistance under the movement of the Spirit of Love.

No human movement is perfect, but the prime author of this approach, Father Gustavo Gutiérrez, with whom I have spoken on several occasions, has taught me to trust that the Spirit of truth and love animates the poor and their companions in this historic struggle for justice. I also benefited from a lengthy personal conversation with Archbishop Oscar Romero's theologian, Father Jon Sobrino, s.j., I recall one of his comments, in which he noted that the peasants of the world know that the battles for justice are paid for by their blood. They are very perceptive and move one cautious step at a time. But they are moving; they will not stop.

Journey to Latin America

I visited Latin America on several occasions. My first visit was with a delegation of the Canadian bishops who had been sent to make the external tour, visiting countries bordering on the oceans. I had an interview with Archbishop Oscar Romero in the simple quarters near the hospital where he lived. He had just returned from Europe and appeared worn out. Louvain University in Belgium had given him an honorary degree. He was less enthused about his encounter with Vatican officials. It disturbed him to realize they had not grasped the difference between liberation theology of Latin America and materialistic theories of Marxism born in Russia.

Romero knew from persistent daily experience that the struggle for justice in El Salvador was inspired and guided by the preferential option for the poor. During the Council, bishops like Brazil's Helder Camara repeatedly entreated the Council Fathers who would listen to stretch out their arms to the poor of the world and to commit the Church to this option. The Latin American bishops achieved only limited success. However, they gathered at Medellín and Puebla in 1968 and 1979, respectively, and committed their local churches to move in this direction. Today they still meet determined resistance from the wealthy and powerful leaders of their regions.

Archbishop Romero was assassinated in March 1980, just after I left his country. He was for the Church in El Salvador a modern martyr, yet he has not yet been canonized. People on Vancouver Island were very generous when I invited them to contribute to a fund in honour of Archbishop Romero. I had been warned not to send money through a bank, as the recipient would become a target for repression. The only safe way was to carry it personally, and even that was not without its dangers. And so I went.

At the airport in San Salvador, a young priest retrieved my luggage, and I offered a special prayer as my guide drove past the checkpoint where some missionary sisters had been apprehended, tortured and killed shortly before. Luckily, no one stopped us. Arriving at our destination, I handed the briefcase filled with donations to Archbishop Romero's successor. He thanked me profusely. I was very proud of the people of our diocese, who had contributed so generously, and I was both delighted and relieved when their gift had been safely delivered.

Shortly afterwards, I received a letter from a bishop in El Salvador, which included these words: "You cannot realize how important it was to learn of your commitment to social justice. Somehow it gives me hope and strength, as it gives hope and strength to others, to learn that there are growing sectors of the Canadian church who are willing to speak out against tyranny and exploitation and stand together with the people who are struggling for social justice."

Social justice continues to be a grave concern for other countries as well. In Guatemala, I met Vicente Menchú, head of the United Peasants' Committee and father of Rigoberta Menchú, the Nobel Peace Prize recipient. Vicente Menchú led a delegation of persecuted peasants coming to plead with the Spanish Ambassador to bring their plight to the attention of the United Nations. The police surrounded the Spanish embassy, set it on fire and killed the peasants. As I listened to a government version of the story the next day on a local radio station, I realized that Vicente was now also a martyr. He had confided to me the previous day that he and his companions were not afraid to die so that their children might have a normal life in the future.

Social Justice at Home

Here at home, the CCCB took part in a coalition called The Working Committee for Social Solidarity, which in 1987 issued a declaration on social and economic policy for Canada. It was titled *A Time to Stand Together – A Time for Social Solidarity*, and it called for groups to unite towards a vision of alternative policies based on social solidarity. Besides the CCCB, other members included the Canadian Labour Congress, the National Farmers Union, and the National Action Committee on the Status of Women. My reputation for allying with such groups and championing such causes earned me the nickname "Red Remi" in some of the local media.

As I worked on and learned more about issues arising from Canada's economy, memories of my life on our Manitoba family farm in Lorne Municipality (section 35, township 5, range 11W) came rushing to the fore, especially when I was invited to speak to the National Farmers Union. This happened on three different occasions: in Edmonton on December 2, 1985; in Vancouver on January 13, 1988; and in Brandon, Manitoba, at the end of July 1989. I collated and read articles in various farm magazines to refresh my own memory and to get in touch with the temper of the times. There is a saying that "you can take the boy off the farm but you cannot take the farm out of the boy." My whole being resonated to the concerns that dominated the delegates' thoughts during these gatherings.

The Edmonton experience proved to be particularly meaningful in returning me to the knowledge of my rural past. As I recalled the principles that the Canadian bishops had expounded through their Social Affairs Commission a few years before, I began to feel an awakening throughout my body of powerful existential feelings from days gone by. I heard myself putting into words feelings and convictions that had lain dormant for years. My remarks focused on three dimensions of farm life that have been evolving over time: agri-culture, agri-business, and agri-power. What I lived during my youth was a true culture and way of life. It has since become more like a business and now even a power struggle. During my childhood and early youth, I had been imbued with a sense of vocation that keeps many farmers tilling the land despite all adversity: they are answering the call to serve humankind by feeding people. For people who are in tune with nature and the environment, and who respect the rhythms of the seasons, there is a mystique about farming. Agriculture is a wonderful way of life.

But in today's world, some people have lost this understanding and have resorted to a manipulation of nature primarily for financial rewards. In a personal conversation at my residence, the Honourable Eugene Whelan, then Federal Minister of Agriculture, described to me the plight of farmers. The family farm was beginning to disappear, as land holdings were radically growing in size. Farmers were losing their options as to what, where and how they could grow their crops.

I regret what is happening to the farmers: they have lost their right to be subjects, agents of their own destiny, not objects to be exploited. Most governments are not sympathetic to farm interests. International speculation controls food markets. Agriculture is being exploited for power, no longer for service. People have been forced off their farms and now face the future without hope.

The reaction of my audience told me I was touching the core of their own experience. Wise farmers know that appropriate nourishment is the very foundation of a progressive society. It is a right that parallels the right to life. Proper farming methods maintain soil fertility and preserve the soil as an irreplaceable heritage. Regressive government policies ultimately endanger the very future of society. Cardinal Newman once penned a memorable phrase: *Cor ad cor loquitur* (heart speaks to heart). The farmers gave me one of the heartiest standing ovations I have ever received.

Three years later, the annual convention of the National Farmers Union in Vancouver, British Columbia, had a somewhat different set of concerns. The title of my talk to them was "Defending Our Farms and Our Future." Here I developed further the three themes of agri-culture, agri-business and agri-power, with specific reference to the then-emerging social solidarity coalition and the ongoing national debate over free trade, with its implications for farmers and agriculture. Once again I had a very sympathetic audience. Agriculture constantly faces ever more grave threats. Here, too, great appreciation was expressed for the fact that a farmer's son, now active as a Church leader, would truly care for them, share some of the same dreams, understand their concerns, and speak resolutely with them and for them in solidarity.

My initiation into modern economics and politics had been a hasty one, done under constant pressure, but it represented a challenge that I thoroughly enjoyed and that has refashioned my entire outlook. These were some of the most productive years for me, as my pastoral talents were constantly refined. I learned to see the bigger picture on a global scale. I discovered that there were two major models of economics. The "competitive" model assumes that inevitably, the fittest will survive as profits and power move into the hands of a deserving elite. The "collaborative" model promotes compassion in both the local and the global spheres of human activity. Work is then seen as humanizing people, not manipulating or exploiting them. We have only to look to the current plight of mother earth and its interlocking chains of events to appreciate how interdependent we truly are.

I feel it is important to remember that after Vatican II, an increasing amount of our work in social action was done on an ecumenical basis. Representatives of the mainline churches met with increasing frequency to exchange experiences, share their insights, pool their resources and profess their solidarity together. As a result, there were years of intense activity where the churches worked together by means of coalitions. I want to render homage here to all the dedicated and very competent people who so willingly gave of themselves to promote the Reign of God in the midst of a rapidly evolving society. I personally received a lot of credit for work that was in good part done by others who were working unselfishly behind the scenes. I am forever grateful to them for their lasting friendship and faithful support.

A Synodal Diocese

Some may wonder why, in my memoirs, I am devoting an entire chapter to the Diocesan Synod held from 1986 to 1991. It was, after all, a local story. Or was it? In fact, the story of our experience represented a microcosm of possibilities for the Church Universal. The seeds that were sown at Vatican II took root and germinated in our diocese as people gathered to reflect on and discern what it meant to be the People of God. Our synod was for me the culmination of my episcopacy and represents my happiest moments as a bishop.

Of course a synod (or "assembly") is not a new thing. An early well-known example of a synod was the Council of Jerusalem, during the Apostles' time. Once Christianity got going as a force in the world, people had to get together to make decisions and settle conflicts, and bishops met for such purposes. Normally, synods were held to address a specific issue, to reflect on the needs of the day and to plan for the future. My understanding and appreciation of Blessed Pope John XXIII's vision and the application of the teachings of Vatican II to my diocese gradually deepened and matured. The revised Code of Canon Law, promulgated in 1983, reflects in part the orientation on which we Council Fathers had agreed. It recognizes the right of bishops to convene a synod in their respective dioceses. Might a synod be held in my diocese? Would it be possible to have a consultative process in the governance of our Church, where not only clerics would be involved but lay people as well?

Looking back, I can trace a pattern of how the story that led to the call to convene a synod began and matured. As a new bishop, I undertook, as I described earlier, contacts with people throughout the diocese, wanting to learn their concerns, joys and hopes, their griefs and anxieties, and to establish various projects that would create a new vision for the diocese. Above all, I was dedicated to implementing a direct application of the spirit and teachings of Vatican II. One of these was to encourage the laity to share their gifts, their experiences and their discernment with the entire Church.

My early pastoral visitations throughout the territory assigned to me helped me get to know the people and share with them the earliest elements of my own vision. This sharing came easily to me. Telling and retelling the Vatican II story was in itself a rewarding experience. We learn from telling our own stories. People everywhere received me with open arms and warm hearts. There was euphoria in the air, aided no doubt by the many news items the mass media had spread around the globe. There was also the faith dimension: Vatican II provided me with a richer insight into liturgy as the "work of Christ" in our midst. Liturgical celebrations were generally still well attended at that time.

The roots of the synod extend as far back as these first years as a bishop. At that time, I distributed a flyer containing 30 questions to all parishes. It had been prepared by a committee of some 20 people – mostly laity, but with some priests and vowed religious as well. We invited everyone who wished to share their impressions of Vatican II: whether the participants had followed the proceedings at Vatican II; whether they were pleased with the results or not; which issues at the Council seemed the most important to them; whether they had changed their impressions of the Church as a result of the Council; whether they approved of dialogue with other religions, other faiths or non-believers; what had strengthened their convictions or changed their minds; what, if anything, had helped them to pray better; what they thought of proposed reforms; how the liturgy could be improved; and in general how they felt as a result of the Council.

The results of this first process, designated the "Victoria Diocese Council Survey 1966," were collated with the use of now obsolete "punch-cards," which simplified and sped up tabulation. The responses provided our diocese with a wealth of information about people's understanding of and reaction to the Second Vatican Council. They mentioned 27 important issues to be further discussed, fifteen different kinds of personal involvement, a variety of comments on recent liturgical changes, and many indications of whether people felt that Vatican II had affected their lives. A fairly detailed overview of current Church life on Vancouver Island emerged from this early contact with the people.

For the next several years, these issues continued to be discussed. I was much inspired and occasionally even moved to tears as I read and reflected on some of the candid comments people put forward. I could feel the movement of the Holy Spirit and the various expressions of divine grace at work in believers' hearts. This privileged contact with the inner life of so many people truly bolstered my own faith and elicited feelings of gratitude that have continued to grow through the years. I became convinced that, for my work as a bishop, I needed not only to consult with lay people and clergy, but also to listen to them as a voice through which the Holy Spirit could be discerned. It heartened me to realize that I was not alone, and did not need to have all the answers, or even all the questions, in order to be the leader of a diocese.

With the benefit of all these experiences as well as an understanding of our Catholic synod tradition, I gradually came to the conviction that the diocese was ready for a further step. After consulting with members of several groups in the diocese, I proposed that we enter into the formal process of conducting a diocesan synod. The idea was readily accepted. It was a direct outcome of the shared responsibility promoted by the Second Vatican Council combined with our own lived experiences of actually seeing this at work in our diocesan structure.

As the idea of holding a synod took clearer shape in my mind, I knew that it could not be conducted in the way we are used to in secular governance, where issues are named, debated and voted on, although some democratic procedures would of course have to be implemented. This was not to be a political encounter or a discussion group experience. It was to be a spiritual experience of communal discernment, an ancient form of prayerful decision making in the Church. Many people who had never before heard the word "discernment" or felt they could not practise it had the surprise of discovering that their habit of calling on God's help in life's experiences and in decision making was actually spiritual discernment at work! Diocesan Prayer Companions offered leadership, and workshops and retreats provided both background in personal and communal discernment and its practice, and the specific application of it to our synod process.

Why was holding a synod so important to me? Vatican II had proclaimed that all members of Christ's body were equal in dignity and in capacity to serve or minister to each other and to society at large. The purpose of our synod would be to examine to what extent the teachings of Vatican II were being lived out pastorally in our diocese and where further improvements might be made.

Proclamation and Storytelling

I chose the 24th anniversary of my nomination as bishop to the Diocese of Victoria – October 31, 1986 – to publish the letter of convocation. The proclamation called for, among other things, spiritual discernment, the establishing of policies for the diocese, reconciliation, and promoting a society of justice and love. It was accompanied by a letter requesting special prayers on the part of those too young to take part, as well as shut-ins, the sick and the elderly. (A copy of the entire document may be found in Appendix II.)

Colleen Mahoney, s.s.a., and her associates guided the synod through three phases: planning an agenda, formulating proposals, and making decisions. It was to take five years to complete these tasks.

It began with storytelling, in which all were invited to talk about themselves and their experience of faith, both personally and within their local communities. Thus the first steps were inward ones. For many people, this was the first time someone had invited them to talk about their own faith experiences as part of an open-ended conversation that did not *have* an agenda but was trying to *find* one.

To bring these issues to the synod, people spent time in personal prayer, then gathered to discern what was a priority. This meant careful listening as well as learning how to put personal agendas aside. Among the participants there grew a bonding and an awareness that they were going to help one another do something about what surfaced as shared concerns.

This is how the agenda for synod developed, growing up from the grassroots. The people, not the bishop, named the issues, and all had equal opportunity to share in the process. From the beginning, all were promised that there would be no censorship, and that they were free to express any opinion. Every item presented was to receive the respect it deserved. Imagine the challenge people had in listening to one another and in respecting one another's wisdom!

Human nature being what it is, we had to come up with ways to make discussion both fair and efficient. Some people love to talk, while others are reticent. Someone came up with the notion of using M&Ms. Yes, those little coloured chocolate pieces became a symbol of our need to give one another a "Maximum of Meaning with a Minimum of Words." With a certain quality of humour, we gave one another M&Ms when we needed to pay more attention to our process and discussion had to be refocused. I like to think that, in this way, we helped one another be more attentive to a true and sensitive practice of discernment. We didn't always succeed fully, but we certainly assisted each other throughout the process, and we experienced a great growth in the ability of the whole community to be a discerning community.

I attended all the meetings. Knowing how some people would always be ready to defer to what the bishop said, I purposely refrained from speaking so as not to influence the deliberations. I chose not to make any intervention during the discussions unless directly requested to do so. This occasioned for me an unusual experience during the synod, and perhaps its most striking aspect. I had known of, but now witnessed in action, the *sensus fidelium* – the gift of faith that lies within the believing community, which I had felt so clearly during some of the sessions at the Vatican Council – alive and well right here in our own diocese. It occurred when, on only two occasions, I was asked for an opinion when the assembly had reached an impasse. To my utter delight, and total satisfaction, each time my suggestion was heard, it was then set aside. No one person, not even the bishop, had all the answers! This, to me, was an indicator of the self-assurance and the maturity that was developing among the participants. When an extreme or questionable proposition was presented, others would inevitably restore the balance. It was obvious from this process that the participants truly felt responsible and free to speak their minds as they saw fit, and had learned that not only their bishop, but they, too, could speak in the name of the Church. I often thought of the saying in some families: "We may not have it all together, but together we have it all!"

I did, however, advise the assembly that any proposals that were beyond our sphere of diocesan competence would be sent to the Canadian Bishops' Conference headquarters in Ottawa, or to the Vatican, for their information. No outside body can correct or change a synod, but they may of course comment as they wish. I got a letter from the Vatican to acknowledge receipt of our activities, but I did not feel obliged to take any "corrective" action.

During the second phase of the synod, we began to formulate proposals. Over 200 were received over the course of two years. They came from individuals as well as from parishes, and from all regions of the diocese. An editing committee sorted through them and placed them in relevant categories, but always without change or modification. The intent of the proposals could be enriched or developed, but could not be discarded. We ended up with 22 dossiers, and the completed proposals were presented to the formal and final synod sessions for affirmation and decision making for the diocesan Church.

In preparation for those final sessions, each parish or faith community was invited to elect or designate three representatives: two adults (one woman, one man) and one young person. These delegates were then invested by me as bishop with a diocesan mandate: they were to attend the meetings and participate with their focus not just on their individual parish or group, but on the entire diocese, considered as one family. All the priests were also entitled to attend, and several did so. A number of other faith groups accepted an invitation to send observers.

As Phase II progressed, an unforeseen but very welcome development occurred. While our meetings had certainly engaged our spirits, emotions and intellects, there had not been any provisions made for our aesthetic sense. A group of artists requested that they might have their own kind of participation, which led to what we designated as a Festival of the Arts. It was sponsored by the Sisters of Saint Ann at their Queenswood Retreat Centre, and produced a wealth of art, some of which was exhibited, demonstrated or performed during the third phase of the synod. There was painting, photography, pottery, poetry, puppetry and music. The local group of Raging Grannies sang about peace issues, a puppet show inspired its audience, and Native dancers from Duncan performed spiritual dancing that represented all of creation. An altar panel of Mary as Raven Woman, pregnant with the Word, was presented by Charles Elliot, a local carver. Altogether, there were 85 performers and 110 artists, and the festival attracted more than 1,000 visitors. The events of the Festival were incorporated into a book to be published in time for the closing of the last session: *Forward in the Spirit: The People's Synod.* The book, which captures the story of the synod, was assembled by Pearl Gervais and Grant Maxwell, who were participants in the synod. They invited all delegates, as well as others who did not attend, to contribute statements that comprise a popular history of the five-year event. Photos of some of the art from the Festival of the Arts are also included in this memorable collection.

Phase III, the final two years of the synod, was the time for decision making and for finalizing directions, making plans and creating a path towards forming the Christian community of the year 2000. Conclusions were reached by consensus as a result of communal discernment. This process was new to many, and surprising to some, for it works on the principle that the entire group must come up with a statement or policy with which all can agree. Even if agreement is not overwhelmingly strong, everyone must say it is something they can live with. Every dissenting voice is acknowledged. When an issue proved too controversial to reach consensus, it was held back for a time of maturing, or else it was set aside until the delegates felt sufficiently at ease with it to proceed further. We learned that this process can slow things down before moving them along, and made us more fully aware of the work of the Spirit in discernment.

During this phase, there began to emerge specific directions that became increasingly clearer as the synod progressed. These directions became indicators of "paths" we would be taking together in forming the future we envisioned. Some of these paths were well beyond our ability to implement, for they concerned directions of the universal Church. Several proposals were put on hold for further study and discernment. I recall two such proposals that generated lively discussion and disagreement. One was "that two mature people in a committed relationship have the blessing of sacrament or ritual to celebrate their commitment to one another." This, of course, raised questions about sexual orientation, divorced Catholics, canon law and pastoral practice, questions that our synod alone could not resolve.

Another proposal "urged the Federal government to pass legislation allowing citizens to direct the military portion of their taxes to peaceful purposes." Again, this went well beyond concerning just the members of the synod, and had enormous implications for our country and for the world. When these proposals came up for discussion, personal biases appeared, political ideologies surfaced, voices got raised, the volume of the discussion rose, people got into the mode of trying to score points, and obvious tension could be felt. It appeared that the whole discernment process would come to a halt. Indeed, it did come to a halt. The facilitator urged the delegates to "take some quiet time in prayer and reflection." People left the meeting space with heavy hearts as well as determination and sadness, wondering what would happen when we came back together again. Even after prayer, reflection and discussion, consensus was still not reached. Each of the participants was invited to let the question rest.

Other proposals and issues reflected and incorporated the tone of Vatican II. On one occasion, I was very moved as I listened to one of our priests speak knowingly and with deep feeling about the situation of people in troubled marriages. He resonated to the pastoral tone of the Council concerning the life situation and afflictions of many couples whose covenant of lifetime fidelity and affection was now in peril for whatever reason. Based on his experience as a caring pastor, he was able to explain clearly how an annulment could help the afflicted partners find renewed peace of heart and mind. He welcomed the new attitude of understanding and compassion reflected in the Council teaching. Now people were offered a second chance to pursue happiness while remaining members in good standing of the Church.

One guest observer remarked that the synod experience is sometimes both walking on water and occasionally sinking, summarizing the feeling of many that "one thing is certain: decision making is not for sissies. It is a rigorous, often heart-wounding process." There were so many times when the variety of emotions and beliefs rose to intense levels over sensitive situations, such as the problems and tensions associated with "mixed" marriages, in which people in "irregular" marriages were deeply hurt by being denied communion, or seeing their children abandoning the Church. Participants poured out their hearts. There were many "aha" moments of discovery and enlightenment as the application of the Sacred Scriptures to current human problems became apparent.

Along the way, there was also a time of profound mourning when a very gifted and beloved priest, Leo Robert, succumbed quickly to an aggressive form of cancer. However, there was a lot of rejoicing as well, as birthdays, anniversaries and special achievements were recognized and celebrated in an increasingly bonded community of friends.

We hired a competent person, Graham Gusway, to help the parishes select and plan their follow-up programs. During our sessions, we were fortunate to be surrounded by the atmosphere of Bethlehem Retreat House in Nanaimo, where they were held. This Benedictine centre is situated beside a beautiful lake, on spacious grounds, allowing for adequate relaxation between working sessions. There was also a popular pub within walking distance for when sessions had finished for the day! Socializing was facilitated and encouraged, and I am certain that many new friendships among the participants endured well past the closing of the synod. One of the more obvious benefits resulting from the synod was that I thereafter sensed that members of our diocese expressed their pride at belonging to our faith community and found pleasure in meeting one another again at other local functions. I found that a much stronger sense of mutual support had developed up and down the Island.

Our sessions always began with prayer, generally starting from a biblical passage relative to the topics under consideration. We often prayed or sang "*Veni Sancte Spiritus*" (Come, Holy Spirit) – an ancient invitation for God's Spirit to be with us – throughout synod, with a deliberate intention to be welcoming and attentive to what the Spirit would reveal in the world today.

Each session also included the celebration of the Eucharist, which happily reminded me of our days at the Council, which always began with community prayer and Mass, followed by veneration and enthronement of the Sacred Scriptures. We used symbols to promote the opening of the heart, mind and body; some found it unusual to insert drums, cedar boughs, movement and art into prayer. At the end of the synod, it became evident that, during our time together, there had been many significant movements in our perceptions, understandings and behaviours. The major shifts, of course, had further dimensions as we began to engage with them in daily practice.

Many Shifts, Many Decisions

We tried to summarize these in some of our decisions. First of all, there was a shift from viewing people for what they have or can do to viewing people as they are, in partnership with one another for the life and development of the community. There was a shift from "doing for" the poor to empowering them and recognizing all persons, however different, as equal, and welcoming and sharing wisdom from the richness of this variety.

There was also a shift from viewing ministry as tasks to be accomplished for others, to viewing it as a life of shared service, grounded in maturing faith. In our notions of education, we perceived a shift from viewing religious education as primarily giving information about faith to a formation in faith for all ages. Spirituality witnessed a shift from viewing it as primarily about religion and church to viewing it as embracing all of life.

Power and authority as an issue for some raised the important question of how to shift from viewing these as the role of one or a few persons to viewing power and authority as the opportunity to empower self and others to accept – and act upon that acceptance – of a full sharing of responsibility in the faith community. This led to a shift in our understanding of how making decisions could be better shared: rather than diocesan, parish or group decisions being made by one or a few, all persons involved in the decision making could learn how to come to consensus. And lastly, we made the shift from viewing structures as a way to maintain and manage the tasks of the community to seeing them as ways to facilitate the evolving development of the community. These were all major transitions in thinking for a great many people; I was delighted to see how they came to be embraced and articulated in our final vision.

Looking back at these changes in our collective perspectives, they do not perhaps seem as radical to me now as they did at the time. This encourages me greatly, for it indicates that what we thought of then as major movements in our collective vision have since become part of our way of thinking and acting, and have proven to be the work of the Holy Spirit.

A synod is "sacred" in the sense that a bishop does not have to answer to an outside authority. He initiates, receives or refuses to receive the results, but he does not "modify" his synod. I proclaimed the Victoria synod immediately. Decisions for Action – 128 of them – arrived at by consensus were promulgated and published. The official promulgation included the commitment of the delegates to journey together in three major areas: developing our faith communities, ministry and justice. This meant we would henceforth work more closely together towards attaining a holistic spirituality, open to the wisdom of other traditions and all of creation. We would support ministry, education and justice in response to the Gospel's call to compassion, conversion and justice, valuing diversity, and supporting each other in working for change.

Delegates gathered with others in the diocese to celebrate the conclusion of the synod, to present its vision, and to provide the fullest possible participation in its promulgation. The final official canonical moment of Promulgation of Synod was at St. Andrew's Cathedral on November 2, 1991. At the close of the synod, the participants declared that our faith community henceforth considered itself a "Synodal Diocese," acting in accord with its unanimously approved Synod Vision:

> We, the Synod of the Diocese of Victoria, reaffirm our belief that we are created in love and called to enter the Reign of God through the mysteries of the Incarnation, Death and Resurrection of Jesus Christ.
>
> Through our common baptism in the Church, the Holy Spirit empowers us to witness to Gospel values and to the wisdom of God revealed in all creation.
>
> We, delegates or participants, commit ourselves to live the vision we have prayerfully discerned, and in solidarity with the oppressed to foster unity with all people of good will.
>
> We invite our sisters and brothers to join us in this quest.

During our five-year synod, I experienced the widest variety of emotions. The initial fear of launching into the deep was there, of making an irretrievable gesture that would commit our diocese well into the future. This shadow of concern was soon replaced by the light of recognition as the work of the Holy Spirit became manifest in the lives of the participants. I sensed the presence of the Risen Christ walking among us on our pilgrim way. I was awed by the beauty of the faith stories people shared in the parishes. It warmed my heart to see people from all over our diocese greet and embrace one another lovingly at each gathering. We were indeed becoming a loving faith family. I trust we will find ways to multiply similar encounters for the continuing benefit of our believing community in its entirety.

Reflecting back on those years of ferment and new initiatives, I marvel at how rapidly many people matured in wisdom and a sense of responsibility. It was a source of great comfort and satisfaction to me as believers claimed their baptismal right not only to belong to their church community but also to "be church" in the fuller sense of the term. Never before had I seen such an awakening to and awareness of the Holy Spirit at work in our midst.

Initially, I was not without moments of apprehension about what people might do with their new freedom to express themselves. Would there be doctrinal deviations and extreme expressions of poorly understood beliefs and practices, destructive initiatives coming from inadequate theological training? Might "ordinary" people be scandalized? Nothing went amiss as far as I could tell. The innate "sense of faith" in the minds and hearts of the people withstood the test. I took real delight in watching people grow spiritually, and regularly gave thanks to God for the abundant grace I saw working in people's souls.

PART THREE

EXPANDING

HORIZONS

8

ADVERSITIES AND LOVE

As in any life, there have been times of extreme difficulty and sadness in mine. It would be an incomplete portrait if I omitted to mention them in these chronicles. During challenging and even hostile times, I wondered if I would have the strength to endure. I have since been asked many times, "How did you survive through all this?" Reflecting on how to answer this friendly query, an image flashed through my mind: I recalled the day when, as a small child, I found myself caught in a gopher trap that I could not open. It was very painful and I was alone. I dragged it home from the pasture to the farmyard where someone helped to release me. I put my injured finger in my mouth to soothe it. Happily, no bones were broken. Life went on as usual. It had become part of me to "tough it out."

One of the earliest prayers I learned by heart was the Russian pilgrim prayer: "Lord Jesus Christ, Son of the living God, have mercy on me, a sinner." I know my own frailty, which I have experienced many times. But I also know that like Abraham and Sarah facing an unknown future, or like Job sitting on his shard heap, or like Jesus in the Garden of Gethsemane, I can always call on my heavenly Father to see me through. With life comes the presence of the Giver of life. Why should I fear? I have been assigned so many major responsibilities in the course of an increasingly long life. Each time, I have found that with the call comes the strength to see me through. The "Our Father" that I have recited countless times invites me to focus on the divine Reign, knowing that God's will ultimately triumphs over all adversities. Heaven knows my weakness, and I can turn to my loving Creator with confidence. And what would I do without true friends whose confidence in me, and whose loving advice, have carried me through many difficult situations? These friends who trust in me and sustain me are priceless treasures for whom I am forever grateful. The road can be, and has indeed sometimes been, long and painful. But the little boy's voice resounds in my memory: "Hang in there – you can do it!" The difference is that today I know that I am not alone.

I have called this chapter "Adversities and Love" because it reflects how, throughout all the difficulties I have had to face, I have also been surrounded and upheld by Love.

A Painful Local Issue

Before my installation as Bishop of Victoria, I had never been anywhere near the city. A friend of mine who had been to the west coast described Victoria to me as a beautiful town where people were not in a hurry and where the sidewalks were rolled up at nine o'clock at night. This idyllic image was shattered by a telephone call I received shortly after I took office. As a brand new bishop, I was drawn into my first major problematic situation.

By nature I am inclined to shun controversy. I try to avoid having to confront people. It came as a shock to me to be caught up in dissension so soon after my arrival. That is one of the dimensions of a bishop's life that I have found most difficult to bear. And yet, why would I expect to live a serene and comfortable existence when others around me are suffering and in distress? People in positions of responsibility know that conflict is part of life. I was aware from past experience that I could expect to have my share. However, it came in totally unexpected ways. I found myself in the eye of a storm of publicity that reverberated around the globe.

This issue involved a small order of nuns, the Sisters of the Love of Jesus, headed by their foundress, Mother Cecilia. She was a convert to the Church who had moved her community from England to Vancouver, and then to Colwood, where they lived in a convent known as St. Mary's Priory. This was also a rest home for the sick and elderly, as well as several stray dogs that Mother Cecilia had taken in. When her term as Superior elapsed, her hobby of providing shelter for a few pets turned into a career; she welcomed more dogs, which now ran unchecked through the rest home. An enlarged shelter hosting a variety of other animals became a source of conflict with her neighbours.

Following several complaints, the Vatican appointed a priest from the mainland, Father Andrew Keber, O.S.B., to investigate the situation and to convey Rome's instructions to me. Mother Cecilia disagreed with the decisions and proceeded to initiate a court case against me, alleging that I was defrauding her community of assets over $1.5 million. Lengthy litigation ensued, but she lost the case. The Court dismissed her claim and entrusted me personally with the assets.

I held a meeting with the Sisters of the community. They agreed that I would set up a trust fund to look after their needs. They also indicated that after their demise, I would be free to use the funds for good works, at my personal discretion. All the Sisters were offered, and accepted, hospitality in other convents, where they would be assured of a stable religious life and security for the rest of their days. Three saw fit to terminate their membership in the community, thereby losing their canonical status as religious.

I appointed my Executive Assistant, Eileen Archer, as well as the successive Diocesan Finance Officers, as signing agents to ensure that the Priory Trust Fund would not be viewed as a source of benefit to me personally. It was kept separate from the diocesan assets to forestall possible rumours that the diocese might be the beneficiary of all these procedures. Eventually, when the Sisters passed away, I decided that the trust would be left to continue building up its investment portfolio in anticipation of future worthy projects.

When Muriel Clemenger became Finance Officer, she continued to make sound investments for the benefit of the fund. Eventually, she approached me with a proposal to purchase some shares in a consortium, of which she was a member, involving Arabian horses. She felt this would be a productive investment for the trust. In view of her previous investment success, I gave her permission to purchase two shares for the Priory Trust Fund portfolio. I understood this would be less than 10% of the portfolio. I would learn later that further sums were drawn from the trust, without my knowledge, to finance the investment in the Arabian horses consortium in the United States. Shortly after, the horse market collapsed and Muriel's investment came to naught.

In due course, Eileen Archer learned about the depletion and brought it to my attention. At that point I spoke with Muriel and expressed my concern. It became apparent to me that she had lost all the monies invested in the horses consortium. I was upset, but she hastened to assure me that she had another project in mind that would recoup the losses from the investment. I was reassured because so far she had succeeded in previous projects. She gave me her verbal assurance that she would not place any diocesan funds at risk.

Muriel informed me that there was a large parcel of property in Washington State, known as the Lacey Lands, which could be purchased at a very favourable price. She was convinced that this piece of real estate held promise for current commercial uses. She was absolutely confident that this land would sell quickly, that the sale would replenish the Priory Trust, and that additional funds would accrue for the diocese. It had always been my policy to trust my collaborators implicitly. Muriel had successfully negotiated a number of real estate purchases for the diocese. I trusted her and approved the purchase of the Lacey Lands. She told me all I had to do was to sign a mortgage guarantee and that all would be well. In hindsight, I realized how credulous I had been in accepting that information at face value.

Unfortunately, that land did not sell as rapidly as my Finance Officer had anticipated. This was where the Lacey land "saga" started. Interest costs continued to accumulate, creating a serious threat for the diocese. I realized in retrospect that I had had a lapse in judgment in not foreseeing the dangers that lurked in this venture. This investment became the subject of litigation when, after my retirement, the diocese defaulted on payment through a decision made by my successor. I was held responsible. The litigations were ultimately resolved in favour of the diocese, but not until very serious allegations were made and high costs were incurred.

Like any responsible captain of a ship, I accepted full responsibility and made this public apology, which was published on June 29, 2000:

> I am deeply saddened by the financial losses which occurred. Ultimately, in my capacity as Bishop of the Diocese, I was responsible for the business decisions which, unfortunately, were unsuccessful. The investments were made in good faith and on the recommendation of the Diocesan financial officer. I had mistakenly believed that there was no significant risk to Diocese assets and that there was substantial equity in the Washington State property.

> This has been a tragic and painful experience for everyone. I apologize again for my errors, as well as the hurt and anguish which my decisions have caused Bishop Roussin, the Clergy and the people of the Diocese.

> While I do not entirely agree with all the statements of the Commission and its process, I do endorse the lessons that are to be learned from this experience. In today's world, it is almost humanly impossible for Bishops to both tend to the spiritual needs of the Diocese and at the same time to be first-class business administrators. I hope that the suggestions of the Commission will form the basis for prudent financial management for all dioceses.

> Finally I want to thank Bishop Roussin and those who are working so hard to restore the diocese's finances. The work that they have done in such a short time is outstanding and I pray that we will all support them to rebuild the faith and financial integrity of the Diocese.

Years later, Muriel telephoned me to offer a verbal apology. I drove over to her residence, forgave her, and we remained friends. Eventually, she put the apology in writing, in a letter dated March 13, 2009:

There do not seem to be words strong enough to convey to you the distress I felt and continue to feel over the serious damage done to your reputation and your ministry resulting from our business dealings ... The fault was mine. It was a very serious miscarriage of all that is just that you were made to take the blame publicly. As we progressed further into the problems with the Lacey land, I failed to keep you in the loop as I ought to have done. I am deeply sorry. Your generous forgiveness when we spoke of these matters has done much to heal. Thank you.

It is only right that you should know that I did make an effort to set the matter straight. When I became aware that Bishop Roussin had made all the business of the Diocese public, I wrote to him, declaring that you were not to blame, that it was I who should shoulder the public censure. I was assured by legal counsel to the Bishop that the letter would be sent to every parish in the Diocese. It was a few weeks before I realized that the letter had not been circulated to the parishes and that the blame was being heaped on you. I made several efforts to get in touch with Bishop Roussin but there was no response. I finally realized that I was of no real importance, that you were the target. In many, many interviews with the media I tried once again to set the record straight, but to no avail. The problems for you went from bad to worse and there seemed to be nothing I could do to stop it ... Be assured of my continuing fellowship in prayer.

Please share this statement with your family and friends.
Sincerely yours in Christ,
Muriel

I never did acquire full knowledge concerning the intricate details of the complex transactions with which Muriel was involved. Later, when she became seriously ill, I invited her to provide me with a written explanation. However, she died shortly after and, as far as I can ascertain, took this information to the grave. At the invitation of her family, I participated in her memorial service.

As Bishop of the diocese, I carried the ultimate responsibility for anything that went wrong. I felt almost totally abandoned and helpless to do anything to remedy the situation. One of the most trying experiences was to see my offer of assistance turned down by diocesan officials. I was completely marginalized and felt somewhat like a pariah.

People have since asked why I remained silent through all this. The simple reason is that I was advised by my legal counsel not to say a word. When this convoluted issue became public, I experienced the darkest, most painful and spiritually trying period of my entire life. Desolation about this case would be my daily companion for several years. I thank God for the constant support provided by a group of close friends.

A local paper had referred to me as a gambler, but to my surprise and encouragement, a member of the diocese countered with, "Yes, Remi is a gambler. He gambled and took the risk: the risk of giving us lay people the responsibility and the confidence to speak out on justice. He helped us realize that we are members of the Church and have responsibilities to be church." I learned a number of hard lessons, but I never regretted trusting the wonderful people who have assisted me over the years.

So many people were hurt, angered, upset and confused over this situation! The diocese was seriously disrupted, and days were spent debating, questioning and formulating responses within parishes and small groups. People canvassed their fellow parishioners, seeking support for bonds the diocese was selling to raise needed funds. This in turn generated even more intense discussion and debate at the parish level and among friends.

Notwithstanding the controversies, the people came forward. I am very proud of them. My own trust was strengthened by the faith and response within the community, investing generously in diocesan bonds. These were later all repaid.

I take this opportunity to share how impressed and gratified I was when I learned how the members of the Victoria Diocese, along with other friends of different faiths, rallied in support. I am truly indebted to them and I thank them all from my heart. By way of example, I signal the generosity of persons like Naz and Jasmine Rayani, outstanding members of the local Muslim community and dear friends, who, I am told, were among the first to volunteer a major donation. They witness to positive interfaith relationships and generosity in action even more than in words.

Those who chose to publicly ally themselves with one side or the other suffered the pain of being misunderstood or having ulterior motives attributed to them. Every person involved in this sad saga ended up being hurt in one way or another. This includes the Benedictine Sisters in Nanaimo, the local *Island Catholic News*, the Diocesan Administration and Muriel herself. I regret very much that my friend Kevin Doyle, an able lawyer whom the Law Society of British Columbia found was wrongly blamed, was drawn into this matter, for I greatly admire his integrity and competence. And I regret the harm to Kevin's professional reputation that ensued.

But love is stronger than everything else, and I am particularly grateful to the religious communities on Vancouver Island – the Poor Clares, the Oblate Fathers, the Benedictines, the Franciscans, the Sisters of St. Ann, the IHM community – as well as the Carmelite Sisters in Hawaii. They continued to pray for the diocese and for me. It was a witness to find them loving yet without attributing blame to anyone. This chapter may come across as my Good Friday experiences, and this indeed they were. However, Easter Sunday followed in God's good time, as it always does, leading us forward to grow in the Spirit of hope and love.

Two Global Issues

The Gospel and the social teachings of the Catholic Church have reminded us of our obligations to those less fortunate. Faith without justice is not a living faith. There are times in my life as well where the interpretation of teachings of either the Gospel or the Church were called into question. Because these have been very instrumental in my maturing as a person and as a Christian, I wish to share two such contemporary issues with you.

My choice is based on the considerations of Catholics today: women's issues, and the possible ordination of experienced married men (*viri probati*, or "elders"). These issues are not only about the on-going struggle of women and men in the Church, but particularly of the institutional Church's struggle with these contemporary dilemmas. The renewal as called for by Vatican II is not an overnight process. It has challenged not only laity but clergy as well. While these events are part of my memoir, the issues they raise are still very contemporary and have deep significance for the future of the Church.

In the 1960s I earned notoriety for supporting the Los Angeles community of the Sisters of the Immaculate Heart of Mary when they ran up against the local cardinal archbishop over their decision to use their own discernment in responding to the Vatican II call to renewal. They became a "test case" for matters of authority and leadership. Ultimately, after years of turmoil and anguish, they decided to become a non-canonical lay and ecumenical community. My support of them led me to be called on the carpet by Vatican officials. One of the officials chastised me and asked why I, a gifted young bishop with a brilliant future ahead of me, would risk my career for the benefit of these women. I sensed at that time (and was correct) that I would never be moved from Victoria, but have not regretted taking the sisters' side in the struggle to make moral choices on the basis of conscience for women – and men – in the Church.

Related to this issue, I was again called to account for what I said at an international convention on "Women in the Church: Challenge for the Future" in Washington, DC, in 1986. In the closing address, I said that I considered the issue of future ministries of women in the church to be of such importance that it required the communal spiritual discernment of the entire Church, not only of the official hierarchy. I raised a question: "With respect to Orders, are the charisms of women who claim that their attraction to ordination is a call of the Spirit, not worthy of testing by the entire believing church?" I went on to suggest that this issue has become a symbol of the "refusal of the church to come to grips with the challenges presented by contemporary society" and presents serious implications for ecumenical dialogue. The talk received an enthusiastic response from the gathering. I was not advocating any specific policy: just raising the question. This was not really anything new: at the Synod on Justice in 1971, Cardinal George Flahiff, CSB, Archbishop of Winnipeg and former Superior General of the Basilian Fathers, had asked that the Vatican set up a commission to study the roles and ministries of women in the Church. Several Canadian bishops had also requested that the Vatican study the issues involved. Other bishops were present when I spoke and found nothing unusual in my presentation.

Among the many responses I received was a letter of support from Cardinal Flahiff dated November 18, 1986. He wrote, "Your address is certainly outstanding, historically and theologically, and so much in keeping with the needs and the trends both in the Church and in society as a whole at this time." The Canadian bishops had taken a variety of actions since 1971, including a request from their conference that the Vatican set up a commission to study issues pertaining to this matter.

Nevertheless, I was challenged and interrogated. I received a letter from then Cardinal Joseph Ratzinger, Prefect of the Sacred Congregation for the Doctrine of the Faith, asking precisely what I had meant to say in four specific references. They are summed up as follows:

1. Whether the feminist proposal for the transformation of a patriarchal church into a discipleship of equals was a high point in contemporary thought;

2. Could the cultural limitations of Christ's disciples inhibit their capacity to transmit certain attitudes integrally to the early church?

3. In view of the imposing body of evidence concerning the cultural conditioning of early church ministry and its developing forms, do we not have reason for reconsideration of our tradition with respect to women in ministry?

4. Might the refusal to face contemporary challenges cause irreparable harm to the Church?

I assured him that I had tried to present honestly the problems we faced. I ended up sending a complete transcript of my actual remarks. In a similar letter to Cardinal Bernardin Gantin of the Sacred Congregation of Bishops, I assured him that I was not promoting a thesis about ordination but "surveying important pastoral issues which we in North America are called upon to face." I said that I hoped he would no doubt agree with me that a discussion of significant pastoral issues can be engaged in without denying fundamental principles of revealed doctrine or calling into question the unity of faith.

Cardinal Ratzinger acknowledged my letter and asked me to come to Rome as soon as possible to explain myself. This was not to be a joyous encounter! I knew I was not alone in finding it galling to be treated like an errant schoolboy on what was supposed to be my "home turf." I was surprised that Cardinal Ratzinger had made no mention of a letter from Bishop Bernard Hubert, then President of the Canadian Catholic Conference, who had called attention to my many years of service to the Church Universal, as well as in Canada. Bishop Hubert stated that on close examination, he had not found anything different in my observations from what other Canadian bishops had expressed at different times and in various places, including the Synods of Bishops in Rome. Bishop Hubert suggested that the investigation be terminated and the file be closed. He went on to say, "I am sure that Bishop De Roo has learned from this experience. I am confident that he will also continue to be frank, honest, a loyal servant of the Catholic Church, in a hierarchical communion both profound and adult." Several other Canadians – such as Cardinals Emmett Carter and Archbishop (later Cardinal) Aloysius Ambrozic, Archbishop Joseph McNeil, Bishop Alex Carter and Bishop William Power –expressed their support on various occasions. This has been one of the greatest sources of comfort for me.

The last "adversity" I wish to include here concerns the possibility of ordaining married men as priests. A lunch I had with Pope John Paul II in 1994 sums up this issue clearly. Many bishops, including me, enjoyed the hospitality of this pope. It was his custom to invite a group of a dozen or more to have a meal with him.

I admired his ready wit, trenchant mind, ease in recalling people's names, and wealth of information garnered from his worldwide travels. We were enjoying an open discussion of all sorts of topics. I was determined that one of them would be the ordination of mature married men. I was sitting next to the Pope, at his right hand. He attacked his food with gusto, pausing occasionally to hold his fork and knife upright in his hands. At one point, I suggested that we might consider the pastoral problems caused by the shortage of priests, particularly in remote areas like the ones represented by most of the bishops who were present at that luncheon.

He ignored my request by glancing to his left. The exchanges moved along; I waited for a second opportunity for a lull in the conversation. This time, speaking in French to make sure he would grasp every word, I carefully but directly faced him with the issue of our people being deprived of the Eucharist. Should we not call to ordination mature married men (*viri probati*) who could provide the spiritual nourishment that was so sorely lacking in areas deprived of clergy? He turned and glared at me, then banged deliberately on the table with his right fist holding the knife handle. In a loud and emphatic tone of voice he declared, "*Deus providebit!*" (God will provide!). That was, sadly, the end of the exchange.

My heart sank as I looked at the other bishops and noted that not one of them dared to pick up on the issue. Where better than in the privacy of his own dining room could we safely and courteously make our wishes known to the Bishop of Rome on such a burning issue? So much for dialogue! We were all aware that the Pope knew that all the other Christian denominations, and other Catholic Rites in communion with Rome, ordained married men. Like other bishops, I accepted ordained married men who transferred from other Christian churches. They are welcomed by our people and minister effectively among them. Why this double standard? Why must this exclusively Latin Rite discipline continue to be imposed, to the spiritual detriment of our people? Why should candidates for ordination not have the option? The celibacy of religious orders is a precious gift and needs to be preserved. Single men are to be encouraged to set this living example. But what about the right of our people to be nourished with the Bread of Life? The Eucharist forms the Church just as the Church celebrates the Eucharist.

Another situation developed in the summer of 1999, when I was invited to address the International Federation of Married Catholic Priests (also known as Corpus USA). I agreed to do so because I believe it is vital for bishops to dialogue with other members of the Church. However, several months before the event, I received a letter from Monsignor Luigi Bonazzi, Chargé d'Affaires in Ottawa, advising me that my presence would be such a great source of "scandal and confusion to the faithful" that I should remove my name from the speakers' list and not attend. In effect, I had been silenced without any discussion. I sent a copy of the letter to the Corpus contact person. The letter was published and several newspapers picked up the story as well. The conference organizers were not surprised by the Vatican's ban on my speaking; some responded by assuring the officials involved that the faithful they associated with were not confused but many were scandalized by the silencing.

In all these controversies, I have been both saddened and disappointed, but I truly do understand where those who disagree are coming from. My speech in Washington said nothing new; my views on how to alleviate the shortage of priests and the presence of married clergy in other rites were hardly revelations. The difficulty arises when disagreeing parties will not enter into dialogue with one another. When "the Emperor has spoken" becomes the final comment of those in power, there cannot be any useful discussion, still less true discernment. But people *can* engage in serious issues maturely without denying fundamental principles of revealed doctrine or calling into question the unity of faith. I share the conviction expressed by Pope Paul VI, in his encyclical *Ecclesiam Suam,* that a condition for fruitful dialogue is to listen to what the other people are saying in their hearts to interpret their meaning in a constructive way. Only in understanding their intent and searching together can real progress be made towards arriving at the fullness of truth.

I hope and pray that people will believe me when I say from my heart that I do not attribute ill intent to any of the people involved in any of these difficult episodes. My motto is "Building in Love." Adverse events had me reflecting and praying on how to keep on loving constructively, living positively for all who surrounded me. In my pastoral work, I am aware that each of us has moments of wondering how we will live through dark times. At those moments of darkness, my faith and my community of friends and family become inestimably important. They are divine gifts, showing me God's loving presence in tangible ways. They, too, were building in love. Whether through prayer, letters, gifts, notes or invitations to dinner or to take a break, through birthday events and celebrations of my anniversaries as bishop, my many friends, nationally and abroad, continue to remind me that their hearts are with me, and their home is also mine.

And so I have been able, in retirement, to continue my work as tirelessly as possible to promote the vision of Vatican II, to speak, whenever occasion allows, to the issues of faith and justice that confront our Church, and to live every moment of every day filled with hope for our collective future.

9

A NEW SET OF TIRES

I retired as Bishop of Victoria in 1999, according to Church law, which states that bishops are to submit their resignation at the age of 75. But retirement does not necessarily mean stopping work! Rather, for me, it meant a "re-tiring," the equivalent of putting on a new set of tires in anticipation of a journey that would carry me many more miles. Although I had enjoyed and been challenged by my over 37 years as resident bishop, I had places to visit, people to meet and more learning and sharing to do. My health was still very good. I felt called to continue my life as a pilgrim of Vatican II.

I sensed it was my duty to continue sharing the renewed vision of Blessed John XXIII with all the people who might benefit from its insights. Thus I decided to consecrate the remainder of my energies to sharing the Council's message whenever and wherever the occasion presented itself, and in any situation where I might receive a hearing. Without any special planning on my part, I have found myself speaking about the Council and sharing some of its concerns with people of good will across Canada, the United States, Great Britain, France and China. The speaking engagements encouraged me to continue reflecting on the vision that had inspired me so much. New insights emerge through these exchanges, and I owe much of my deepening understanding to this process, and to these requests from the grass-roots, for which I am very grateful.

Interest in the Council remains real and current. People of many lands welcome firsthand reports from a Council Father who attended all four sessions and was immersed in the process from the moment in 1959 when Pope John XXIII announced his intention to convene it. Despite the comments from some that "Vatican II is dead!" others are keeping its vision alive and looking for creative ways to keep implementing it. People from all sectors want to hear about it, and the Spirit is moving still.

Not all of my travelling has been to speak on Vatican II. It has been possible for me to reconnect with my ancestral roots in Europe and the United States as well. My friends Marie Therese Van de Voorde and her husband Remi Lamal helped me to establish some of these contacts in Belgium, beginning in 1950. John and Mary Virginia De Roo later expanded the US contacts. The scope was broadened internationally by the diligent research of genealogist Patrick Deroover and his spouse, Hilde Bourgoy. This led to the publication of De Pape (2005) and De Roo (2008) family trees, which date back to the 12th and 15th centuries. We celebrated memorable international family reunions in Belgium and Portugal.

There have been other memorable encounters, one of which was in Paris in the summer of 2007. I had first seen the magnificent Cathedral of Notre Dame when I was a young priest on my way to Rome for doctoral studies. It was an awe-inspiring sight, but never would it have crossed my mind that someday I would return there for the experience that follows.

Friends and I were touring in Paris when we noticed a sign near the cathedral inviting people to register in advance to qualify for free tickets to attend the Solemn First Vespers, followed by a cruise on the Seine River and a Pontifical Eucharist marking August 15, the national feast day of the Assumption. The administration needed a head count to reserve the required number of boats, or *bateaux mouches*, to accommodate all the passengers. We signed up for the event and returned the next Saturday, ready to participate. On approaching the cathedral, we took note of the long row of tourists waiting for admission. I invited my two friends to come with me to the head of the queue. I then told the officer in charge that as a guest celebrant, I needed immediate access in order to get vested. With his consent I motioned to my friends to enter directly while I proceeded to the sacristy to obtain the required liturgical garb.

Once attired, I stood among the large group of clergy and religious fraternity members awaiting the signal to proceed. As the organ began to play, I noted that the chief celebrant was nowhere to be seen. Then, out of the corner of my eye, I saw the Dean of the Cathedral and the Master of Ceremonies rushing towards me with a crozier and ceremonial book in hand. "Bishop," they exclaimed, "would you please preside?" I would later discover that the Cardinal was away at an International Youth Congress in Cologne, Germany, and that due to a misunderstanding, the auxiliary bishop who would normally replace him had not yet arrived. (He did eventually arrive an hour later.) Imagine the look on the faces of my two companions waiting inside when they saw me walking at the end of the long line of vested participants, blessing the crowds, ascending the pontifical throne, and then intoning the opening hymn for vespers in French as the "substitute" Archbishop of Paris!

"China Is My Mother"

But most of my travelling has continued to be about telling the story of the Council. I have criss-crossed North America from east to west and north to south, and have travelled abroad as well. Of all my experiences, my contacts with China have been one of the most enriching of my life. They centre in a special way on the prophetic figure of Aloysius Jin Luxian of Shanghai. Still alert in his late 90s, he has led an extraordinary life. He has spent a quarter of a century in various forms of detention, ranging from house arrest to imprisonment and even solitary confinement. Through all of this he has remained a man with a resilient sense of faith and a truly compassionate heart. He is fluent in half a dozen languages, has travelled widely, and has friends in many countries. One day he reminded me that while he respects all of the ten commandments, he has developed a special understanding of the fourth commandment. It embraces not only his parents but also his country: "China is my Mother," I once heard him exclaim. He serves the Church loyally, and is also a staunch supporter of his own country, particularly in its current period of transition.

Inspired by his leadership, countless lay people in Shanghai have risen to the challenge of modern ideologies. They openly profess their faith, and we are very aware of how much they love their country and their God. There is a story here that I take great pleasure in relating, using pseudonyms for reasons easily grasped.

"John" and "Joseph" were having lunch. In the course of the conversation, John looked at Joseph and said, "You seem to be different from most of the other business people I know. You are very successful at your work, you seem to be without worries, never preoccupied, so much at peace with yourself, so buoyant and happy. Why is that? Can you tell me why?" Joseph reflected a moment and responded that, as far as he knew, he did the same work under similar conditions as did John, and did not feel he was exceptional. Both men made good money, had a loving wife and a family with the prospect of a secure future. However, his companion continued to probe. Finally, Joseph said, "I am a Christian."

"I never heard of that," responded John. "What does that mean? A Christian? What is that? I want to be like you!"

The sequel to that exchange was that Joseph introduced John to his wife Mary, who had taken it upon herself to tell others, when asked, about Christianity. In time, John asked to be baptized Catholic. Mary made arrangements for John's baptism with one of the few available priests. This appears to be typical of the way in which lay people in parts of China have assumed their responsibility for the spreading of the Reign of God in that immense territory, a land rich in culture but starving for spiritual nourishment. This story reminded me very much of the early Church.

China is, in many ways, a blossoming of the modern world with which the Church must associate. During my youth on the farm, I had entertained the strangest notions about China. All I knew at that time was that there was a Chinese restaurant in a nearby town. But I had never had a conversation with a person from China.

For many people, China remains a country shrouded in mystery. I am inclined to agree with a comment I once heard about this great and populous land: someone who has been to China once may be tempted to write a book; the person who has been there twice may be content with a well-considered article; but the third time around, one will probably prefer to keep silent.

But I do not wish to keep silent about my own insights into this immense country, which are offered here with some hesitation. Three short visits is very little time to observe and absorb the complexities of this ancient culture. It was once suggested to me that any information about China that originates outside the country itself has to be considered with great discernment. So many superficial labels have been attached to the people. Many of those I met were obviously very sensitive about what was being said about them. On my first visit in 1986, I found a China that lagged far behind us. Very few cars, many old trucks filled with workers, all dressed alike in their muted blues, drab greys and Mao caps, resigned looks on their faces. Today we walk past huge supermarkets where milling crowds examine the latest electronic gadgets and endless lines of cars dash back and forth in a maze of noisy traffic. Our own driver was part of the fray, jostling to and fro in his late-model car, unperturbed by the other vehicles bustling about him, adjusting his two cell phones from one ear to the other as he responded to a constant flow of messages, all the while entertaining us with bits and pieces of valuable information.

On two occasions, Bishop Jin invited me to lecture on Vatican II to his seminarians, the women religious of the diocese and some of the priest professors. For one week, in a series of five two-hour sessions, and speaking through an interpreter, I shared some of my memories of Vatican II, focusing on the doctrinal highlights and the renewed pastoral insight I received from these four intense years of working with bishops from around the world. Though the participants' response was somewhat muted by their very limited fluency in English, we seemed to understand one another quite well. I was truly inspired and encouraged by what I learned and saw there.

On the third trip, after my four lectures, I invited my co-worker Pearl Gervais and my youngest sister, Madeline Martinez, to give the talk on the baptismal priesthood of laity. By having lay people teach on this subject, I avoided giving a clerical perspective and tried to illustrate to my audience how lay people are coming into their own since Vatican II.

One of my most memorable experiences was joining with Bishop Jin for a Month of Mary pilgrimage at the renowned sanctuary of Our Lady of Sheshan, about an hour and a half drive from Shanghai. It was May 1, 2008, also the great feast of Chinese Workers, and a national holiday. Smiling uniformed guides and guards waved us on as our car made its way through the milling crowds, past a checkpoint, then directly into the narrow roadway leading up the mountain to the basilica and its sanctuary. Several thousands of pilgrims from various parts of China came to pray to their Mother Mary. I felt honoured to stand in solidarity, as a representative of the Western Church, with these admirable sisters and brothers in Christ who continue to plant seeds of faith and hope in an oppressive environment. As we processed out, imagine my utter astonishment, at this very solemn event, at hearing the tune "Old Black Joe" sung with spiritual lyrics, as if this Negro spiritual were calling forth a new liberation in a foreign land.

The glossy Rome-based Magazine *30 Giorni* (30 Days) featured a long and beautifully illustrated article covering the event. In one of the pictures, I am shown assisting Bishop Jin at the altar during the "great elevation," holding aloft the chalice. I was profoundly moved as the many implications of this situation stirred my heart and mind. How significant that a bishop from the Western world could stand side by side with his brother in faith in a land where religion was once bitterly suppressed. On two occasions I was privileged to take part in this public proclamation to the world that the faith Bishop Jin and I both cherish is still alive in China!

The local people cautioned me to be very circumspect when it came to news releases and various articles that do not originate from within China itself. Many vested interests come into play under the complicated circumstances. The intense persecutions are at last somewhat alleviated, but more subtle forms of pressure are brought to bear on people of faith, in various ways. We are all urged to keep the Christians of China in our hearts and prayers. I encourage visits to China, provided they are not simply touristic ventures, but rather a reaching out to our sisters and brothers who are pioneering new pathways of faith in a rapidly evolving world, still as mysterious as it is fascinating and even attractive.

During my second and third visits to Shanghai, I was invited to preside at Eucharist in several parishes. Some were strictly Chinese communities, while others were mostly expatriates who understood English. I felt quite at home in their midst. There was always a joyful, even festive, mood in the congregations. They sang with great gusto. After Mass, my companions and I always made a point of greeting the people as they left the church. I was astonished at the variety of countries from which they came, and there was plenty of youth and vitality in the groups. They were very happy to have visitors and pleaded with us to come back again.

Lay people have reclaimed almost half of the several hundred churches that were confiscated during the Revolution. That in itself is a major challenge. Everything had been lost, including such things as precious vessels and the statues that once adorned the churches. I was shown a statue of the Sacred Heart that a non-Catholic had reconstituted using a series of sketches based on the memories of older people. Having no sample to show, the plaster casting had to be repeated three times before the people were satisfied that it looked like the "real thing."

My companions and I were also the guests of a number of well-educated lay people who are deeply engaged in Church life. I found the believers that we met to be solidly attached to their faith and to the Church. All spoke with great respect of the Pope. The process of reconciliation with the Vatican already bears rich fruit. It was evident to me that there is a profound longing for more visible unity with the

Bishop of Rome and for contacts with other Catholics around the world. The people I have met in China are also proud of their country, despite all the persecutions people have undergone, and the constraints they still have to endure.

In mainland China, local Catholics generously offered to serve as tourist guides, which allowed me to hear and see through the eyes of local people the rich culture and history of their homeland. What a privilege to experience the pride and hope of the people! One of my most memorable visits was in Beijing, to the tomb of Matteo Ricci, a sixteenth-century Jesuit who used Chinese language and customs to explain Christianity. Bishop Jin had written a book about Ricci as a way to share a rich aspect of Church history in China and to introduce a significant model for his flock. Sister Mary from Shanghai accompanied my companions and me. She was ingenious in finding whatever we needed. A volunteer guide gladly showed us the old graveyard where several tombstones of former missionaries have been preserved. Ricci's influence on China has been profound, and Christians there have a model to look up to and a positive experience of enculturation. It is left to our imaginations to wonder what a difference it would have made if other missionaries had followed Ricci's example of respecting and enriching the local culture instead of imposing European patterns of worship and Gospel proclamation.

To visit China is also to visit Taiwan and Hong Kong. In Taipei, Taiwan, Wilfred Chan, s.j., showed us the Catholic educational facilities as well as the highly respected Catholic hospital. We also saw how the apostolic endeavours of the Jesuit Fathers are bringing the Good News to various sectors of society. I admired how the missionary community of the Society of the Divine Word (S.V.D.) Fathers had combined their efforts with those of the local government to provide housing and sustain several forms of social work. Here, too, the Gospel message was seen to bring about an improvement of living conditions. The tiny percentage of Catholics in the population is having an impact far beyond their numbers and is proving how the Christian message contributes to the humanization of the citizens. Archbishop Ti Kang (now retired) shared with us a number of stories illustrating how the Council teachings are having a constructive influence.

The Sisters who run a hospital there invited us to present a workshop on "Biblical Characters and the Enneagram" to their professional staff. (Our book of the same name has now been translated into modern Chinese and appears to be quite popular.) The renewed interest in modern disciplines like the Enneagram makes it possible to better understand the workings of grace in the human psyche while it enriches our understanding of spiritual relationships. Contrary to some impressions, the Vatican's recent document on the New Age does not "condemn" the Enneagram, a popular system of personality types partly developed by Jesuits in the United States and widely used in Catholic retreat houses. It is a valuable aid to spiritual growth when it recognizes the Divine centre of each person, and I have found it invaluable in understanding my own spirituality as well as that of others.

A "Pilgrim of Vatican II"

Since my retirement, I have also continued my concerns for the people of El Salvador. Every year, there is a memorial service for Archbishop Romero in one of the downtown churches in Nanaimo, where I presently reside. I have repeatedly been asked to be a guest speaker at this event. Sadly enough, there has been prolonged hesitation in the Vatican to promote the cause for recognition of Romero's sainthood. One wonders about the motivation behind this reticence. His own people moved without hesitation to erect a memorial on his tomb in the Cathedral. I see there an example of spontaneous recognition of their former pastor as a hero and martyr for the faith. The people themselves are repeating the ancient custom of spontaneous acclamation. There has been an incessant flow of pilgrims who come to honour him. I have observed this on more than one occasion, and have drawn great strength from his memory and my former association with him. Pope John Paul II stopped to venerate his memory by praying at the tomb in the course of his travels. In many worship services I have attended, people called out the names of former associates who had died in the cause of proclaiming the Gospel and struggling for justice.

The congregation would exclaim *"Presente!"* (Here with us!). I have thus been frequently reminded of Romero's declaration: "My enemies may kill me but I will rise again in my people."

Another favoured place since my retirement is Hawaii. A fortuitous encounter with two Chinese Carmelite Sisters in the 1970s led to a development I could never have anticipated. For the past ten years, they have invited me to co-facilitate a yearly retreat of eight to ten days for their small community in Kaneohe, near Honolulu. They choose from a variety of proposed topics. We have become very good friends in the process and all look forward to each renewed event. I have been greatly enriched through this exposure to Carmelite spirituality.

As well, an association of Hawaiian lay people, the Big Island Liturgy and Arts Congress (BILAC), hosts extended workshops each year at Chaminade University, operated by Marianist brothers, in Honolulu. Artists come to share their talents in music, art, song and dance. They contribute to high-quality liturgies throughout North America and beyond, and invite me regularly to help them benefit from the insights of Vatican II.

Across the other ocean, I felt greatly honoured when I was invited to speak at a symposium in England in memory of Bishop Christopher Butler. The symposium, which was organized in October 2002 by lay people in England, focused on the Vatican Council teachings. I consider Butler the most eloquent of the English-speaking Council Fathers, as well as forthright and courageous. We became very good friends and had several opportunities to discuss issues affecting our Church.

During the Council, I also got to know some of the Belgian scholars fairly well. Their influence far outweighed their numbers, and I have maintained occasional contact with the University of Louvain. And in Paris, at St. Gervais and Protais Church, I was delighted to discover that the Sunday liturgy is preceded by an hour of meditation, and the church is full!

Closer to home, significant initiatives are keeping the vision of Vatican II alive. In Arizona, I spoke to the Jesuit Alumnae of Arizona (JAAZ) group; in Milwaukee, to the Call to Action organization; and to

Faith and Sharing groups in Portland, Oregon. At St. Patrick's Church in Seattle, the big feasts are celebrated with liturgical dance and song. The hard of hearing and the mute use sign language in the assembly so all can join in the Lord's Prayer together. On Vancouver Island, Faith and Sharing groups that are caring for people with disabilities and their families are promoting a renewed vision of the Beatitudes. The Ranaghan Media Centre in Calgary, an ecumenical centre that offers daily programs on the radio and Internet to promote contemporary issues and solutions for spiritual life, interviewed me twice. The National Center for the Laity in Chicago continues to implement Council teachings in many areas, including business, spirituality, labour and liturgy. Laval University in Quebec City has a department devoted to the promotion of Vatican II, and I was a participant in one of their symposiums. Saint Paul University in Ottawa recently launched its Research Centre on Vatican II and 21st Century Catholicism. I was invited to take part in its 2012 symposium on Vatican II for the Next Generation.

Young people are asking questions, professors are writing and publishing about the Council, and the public at large comes out to hear me, a museum piece as a Council Father, hoping to leave with renewed hope and joy. To my delight, they express boldness and compassion for themselves as part of the People of God.

The ecumenical experience I enjoyed during the Council encouraged me to help found, in partnership with the Anglican and United Churches, the Centre for Studies in Religion and Society at the University of Victoria. The Centre has collaborated with initiatives spearheaded by lay people of the diocese and enjoys broad ecumenical and interfaith support. I have repeatedly been invited by other Christian churches to speak on topics related to Vatican II, a constant reminder of how the Council has profoundly transformed the mentality of many other churches and has improved the quality of our interrelationships.

Vatican II also significantly influenced contemporary church architecture. In three of the churches where I participated in liturgies during retreats, lectures or workshops, I was happily aware of the participation of the faithful taking part "knowingly, actively and fruitfully" (as prescribed by the Constitution on the Sacred Liturgy, in a translation by Walter Abbot, SJ). At a retreat in Calgary, Alberta, I was moved when the story of St. Michael's Church was told to me. Here was a place of worship built on the foundation of Gospel and Vatican II teachings. The parish had assembled, planned and made of their church building a witness to a believing, joyful Church. In it, all are welcome. There is a safe space for children, places for people with disabilities, for musicians, for street people to shower and be fed, and a spacious area for the community at large to celebrate passages of joy and sorrow.

Everywhere, I have found continued interest in, though not always concrete evidence of, local initiatives that are inspired by the spirit of the Council. The one group I wish to identify for special recognition is the communities of religious men and women. The Council urged renewal, going back to their sources. Religious men and women took this very seriously. They reflected on their founders' lives and works, they reclaimed their vision, they read the Gospels, and they discovered anew the Beatitudes, their baptismal priesthood, and their privilege of constituting the Church.

As a guest at a provincial meeting of the Sisters of St. Joseph of Carondelet in Los Angeles, I witnessed those Sisters, and hundreds of their lay associates – both men and women – discern their future together as equals. The organizers also included their elderly and re-tired members by streaming in the proceedings and having "virtual" discussions. These Sisters, too, were discerning how best to support their active members. Most of the women's congregations I have spo-ken to also have specific projects for social transformation. Further east, the Sisters of St. Ann in Marlboro, Massachusetts, invited me, as a Council Father, to keep even their older members informed about the teachings of the Vatican Council. The respect shown to the elders as bright, competent women despite their age moves me. They pray, yes, but they also are present in the wisdom they share with the uni-verse. While age is gradually catching up with them and eroding their resources, they have left an enviable record of social engagement in the transformation of society.

More recently, other communities – such as Romero House in Toronto (founded by Mary Jo Leddy), the Emmaus Community on Vancouver Island, as well as L'Arche communities founded by Jean Vanier – reflect the vision of Vatican II as they respond to the signs and needs of the times. I have been enriched and heartened as I witness their hope and love.

I find I am just as busy today as I was while in office, only the scope of my work has taken on a broader field of vision. My participation in workshops, lectures and retreats has allowed me to witness firsthand what Jesus called "the signs of the times." When people ask me whether I find travel difficult, and how I handle it, I simply reply that I keep telling the story to whoever will listen, wherever they are. The story is that of Vatican II, its ongoing impact, and its vision of hope for us and for the future of our Church.

On my website I describe myself as a "Pilgrim of Vatican II." For the rest of my life, this pilgrimage will be a priority for me. Obviously, not every parish has fully embraced the prophetic vision of Blessed Pope John. But the New Pentecost he confidently predicted, and that his successors repeatedly recognized, continues in its quiet way to transform our world. The ways of the Lord are not restricted by human frailty or opposition. I will never miss an opportunity or turn down an invitation to share with others the monumental and historic event that has brought such a powerful and imperative call for renewal into our Church. All in all, I can affirm from my own experience that the influence, the "spirit" or deeper insights of Vatican II, continues to bear fruit. The Holy Spirit is moving, regardless of outward appearances. It is blowing with divine freedom, and penetrates all walks of life, sometimes where we least expect it.

10

THE FUTURE BECKONS

To a historian, 50 years may well appear as but a moment in time. To a frail human being, it is a substantial part of one's life. As I look back on my half-century as a bishop, time both collapses and expands as my experiences seem so distant and yet so immediate. Working on these chronicles, I became much more aware of the passing of time; I reflected frequently on how Vatican II, and my participation in it, fit into the greater life of the Church. Fifty years after its closure, Vatican II is still in the early stages of what is known as "reception," the process whereby the members of the Church receive, recognize, accept, make their own and apply to daily life the official teachings of the Church. The Council is part of a continuing process of renewal, both of our Church and of ourselves as its members. Our hopes, dreams and challenges are caught up in this dynamic.

The Council led me to embark on a personal journey into my past, beyond the institutional or legal dimensions of Church life, into the realm of the Spirit present in all people and all things. The flames of faith were stirred up and brought to renewed luminescence. The spent ashes were reverently brushed aside. I was, as St. Paul said, "putting away childish things" while at the same time rediscovering the wisdom of the Word and the Holy Ones who had gone before me. The reality of the New Jerusalem was rising in the dawn of this new era. I was thrilled to be a part of it.

For my early morning prayer period, I like to wrap myself in one of the knitted woollen shawls with which I have been gifted by my First Nations brothers and sisters. They also gave me a black Cowichan sweater carrying my personal coat of arms. They serve me well on cooler days. Such presents have become symbolic for me. I am reminded of the countless gifts that have been showered on me and on our Church that have enriched each one of us. My purpose in writing this book has been to share with others some of the graces, the divine life, bestowed on me during a lengthy life of service to Church and country. I begin this closing chapter with thoughts and feelings of deep gratitude, for my life and for those who have been a part of it.

These chronicles are offered as my personal gift to you who honour me by reading my life story. To my Catholic brothers and sisters, I welcome you to join me as we recall one of the greatest events in the life of our Church. I trust you will appreciate more fully what a blessing Pope John XXIII brought to us when he convened this extraordinary event, which provides us with a compass into the future. To the members of other Christian persuasions, I greet you as fellow pilgrims in our calling as disciples of Christ Jesus and participants in his Paschal Mystery, his life, death and rising. To any baptized believers who have distanced themselves from our present institutional framework for whatever perceived failures, let me assure you that Christ has never left you. He still embraces you in his love. He invites you to be reunited with us. To all people of good will, I urge you to consider the open invitation that the Church extends to you, to join with us in the common pursuit of truth, of peace and of justice with compassion. Without exception, we all share the call to humanize society.

I am convinced that Vatican II has lasting significance for everyone. It offers wisdom and guidelines to help us read the signs of the times and to facilitate the coming of the Reign of God throughout the world. I have sought to present this prophetic Council to you from a pastoral perspective. My desire is to focus on the work of the Holy Spirit, which animates and undergirds its perennial vitality.

The Legacy

What do I see as constituting the legacy of Vatican II? What remains pertinent 50 years later as we contemplate the contemporary pastoral scene?

Foremost in my mind is the way the Council focused our attention on the Mystery of the Church and on the Person of Jesus Christ. This may not seem extraordinary today, but at the time, many people could not shed the idea that the Church was identified with its outward and more visible aspects: the institution, its structures, the hierarchy. To move beyond that to understanding it as the Body of Christ, with Jesus at its head, was to answer the question "Church, who are you?" in a re-energized way. The Council led us to consider the centrality of Christ and to appreciate more fully the role of the Holy Spirit. Now we see that the foundation of our faith is not primarily a book, not a teaching, not an institution, but the living Revelation of God: Jesus abiding in our midst. What is essential is our relationship with the person of Christ Jesus, who is both Message and Messenger. In him alone does our faith find its origins and its perfection. So another way to answer the question "Church, who are you?" is to say, "You are the visible presence of Christ among us and in the world."

To facilitate reflection on the Person of Jesus, I propose two of my favourite passages, found in articles 22 and 45 of *Gaudium et Spes,* The Church in the Modern World. Much of their inspiration for me lies in the reminder that Jesus is the model of the human. He worked with human hands, thought with a human mind, acted by human choice, and loved with a human heart.

Closely linked with Jesus Christ is his mother, Mary, who played a crucial role in our salvation. I was one of the majority of bishops who voted to place our teachings about the Mother of God within our text on the Church. Mary is not above the Church, but within it, our sister and our model in faith as well as our mother and intercessor. In her powerful inspired words of the *Magnificat,* we find a strong woman, praising God from the depths of her heart as she proclaims that the powers of evil will be vanquished and the lowly exalted.

We Council Fathers, after laborious debate, decided to place the chapter on the laity ahead of the one on the episcopacy. Great symbolism was attached to that decision. Recognizing the giftedness of all the baptized also affirms that there are a variety of ministries, not just those resulting from ordination. This understanding calls forth the manifold responsibilities and the need for a full awareness of the laity in their role of building up both the Church and the world. They are, in the words of *Apostolicam Actuositatem* (On the Apostolate of the Laity), truly sharers in "the priestly, prophetic, and royal office of Christ," and they "have their own share in the mission of the whole people of God in the Church and in the world" (AA 2). When facilitating retreats for men ordained to the ministerial priesthood, I remind them that they have a special responsibility to help all the others develop their royal baptismal priesthood. It is foundational to all other ministries.

Another aspect of the legacy entrusted to the laity as well as the clergy was the call to perfect holiness. During my seminary days, the topic of mysticism was approached with caution. We used the term sparingly to describe saints of long ago. Returning to our sources of the ancient Christian meditative tradition, and discovering that believers have experienced mysticism throughout the centuries, was another awakening. Along with it came a deeper awareness of "divinization," a concept that the Eastern Church has always held dear, and that is found in the writings of ancient saints. There is nothing more central to a fuller understanding of baptism and confirmation than this call to the divinization of all that is human.

We hear an echo of this point at Mass, when water and wine are mixed together in the Eucharist as a reminder that we may "come to share in the divinity of "Christ, who humbled himself to share in our humanity." This is ecclesial mysticism, which is not solely found in individuals: it is also a unitive collective experience of the entire Church, in word and sacrament. The warning attributed to the late theologian Karl Rahner is ever present in my heart: the Christian leader of tomorrow will of necessity be a mystic. In the questions people often raise at my Council lectures, I have sensed an awakening of this mystical dimension, which used to be considered the preserve of vowed people who were advanced in the spiritual life. Those religious communities truly gave us an example of how to apply the insights of Vatican II, returning to their roots, updating their various ministries and further developing their heritage. There is nothing more central to a proper understanding of baptism and confirmation than this call to the divinization of all that is human, and I am struck by the joy and hope that light up in people's eyes as they begin to understand and practise this call.

In addition, I find life and sustenance in one of the areas most dear to my heart as a Christian: namely, prayer and liturgical worship. It is through our services, our praising God and our coming together as community that we receive the strength and motivation to live the Gospel in the world around us. I have received very positive reactions from audiences when I remind them that the liturgy is no longer to be understood as a series of practices intended primarily to gain a place in heaven at the end of one's life. When I was a youth, many people left me with the impression that they attended church services more out of fear of damnation than out of the conviction that they were saving the world with Christ. More stress was laid on the obligation to "hear Mass" than on the proclamation of its message beyond the doors of the church, the sending out on mission.

The legacy of a renewed liturgy, embracing the totality of our spiritual life, has broadened our understanding of our call to share the work of Christ in his service to the world. I often wish that every one of us would take this mission to heart. How enriched our lives would then become, centred on the Paschal Mystery of life, death and new life. I find that looking at the cycles in nature is a constant reminder of that mystery, as the seasons repeat the pattern of apparent death and very real rebirth.

I believe that the change of attitude by our Church in its relation-ships with the world was another of the most significant developments during the Council. By this turning towards the world, a new era began. The very thought of an open church caused considerable dis-sension among the bishops. When the Council spoke of the "joys and hopes" of our age, some felt such a statement about the world was too optimistic. For them, the world was in a very dark space. Happily, the positive position was maintained, and we can continue to proclaim with enthusiasm that joy is present in the whole of creation, the joy that, according to Teilhard de Chardin, is "the most infallible sign of the presence of God."

Ecumenism and interfaith relations were other areas where much was accomplished. Great credit is due here to the personal example and leadership of Pope John XXIII. His friendly attitude and his respect for people were contagious. He encouraged the Council Fathers to use the medicine of mercy rather than that of severity to heal our rifts and divisions. One non-Catholic friend said to me, "John XXIII is the best Pope we Protestants ever had!" I love the story of his encounter with a group of Jewish rabbis who had come to the Vatican for the first time ever. He had them seated in a circle of which his own chair was a part. Then he welcomed them with these words: "I am Joseph your brother." I believe that gestures of this kind were among the reasons why non-Catholic observers accepted his invitation to attend the Council. The stage was set for promising new developments.

The Future

I have frequently referred to myself as a pilgrim of Vatican II. At the close of these chronicles, I reiterate and underscore this phrase. My participation in the Council and living in its aftermath have been truly fulfilling experiences. Vatican II enriched my life by deepening my faith and increasing my sense of reverence and awe in contemplating the divine plan of salvation. I now see the Church primarily as mystery, a humble and graced pilgrim People of God, and secondarily as an institution and historical structure. The Council brought me to more deeply appreciate my dignity as a baptized member of the Body of Christ, sharing in the universal royal priesthood. My ministerial ordination further calls me to assist all the baptized to live their own basic priesthood of proclaiming the Gospel. I am a "priest for the priests." Our baptism calls us to offer the totality of our being and doing, as sacrifices inspired by the Spirit, made spiritual, so that even "outsiders" may come to worship the true God.

History shows that Councils have coincided with periods of upheaval, and there is reason to believe the disturbances already prevalent
in our time will not soon abate. Younger generations are walking away
from many of our churches, and some people even find questions of
faith irrelevant to their everyday worlds. There will also be those who
are prisoners of yesterday. They live in a world of the past. They seem
to have lost hope. We need to love them into wholeness. In a world
changing with a speed that few people can imagine, it should not
surprise us that many resist the unknown and fear that which they
cannot understand. It is normal for us today to live in the midst of
constant tension.

There are no simple answers to the complex issues that seem to
be awaiting us around every new corner. Simple answers to complex
questions can cause more harm, only deepening the confusion. It
would be misleading, and less than honest, to suggest that anyone has
all the answers. In fact, today it seems more important to raise the right
questions than to pretend there are easy solutions.

I still meet many people who bemoan all the negative things that
are happening. Evil is real and active, and it is futile to deny this and
wish that somehow evil would evaporate through some miraculous and
instant procedure. But I also meet countless people who have identified themselves as Vatican II Catholics, trying in their own lives to live
out its message. They are among the many signs of hope I encounter.

Certain passages in the Sacred Scriptures have a special resonance
for individuals. For me, one of these is in Chapter 14 of John's Gospel.
Jesus is talking to his disconsolate disciples, who are downhearted
because he is leaving them. But Jesus reassures them by promising to
send them help. With the imparting of the Holy Spirit, he says, they
will accomplish "even greater things." We may well ask: How might
this be? What works must we be about? Where must our energy go?
With whom shall we engage in these "even greater things"? How do
we keep the spirit of the New Pentecost alive? That same Holy Spirit
truly enlivened what I have called the "slumbering giant" that, until
recently, represented the People of God. That giant has been roused,

and as it awakens even more fully, we can indeed expect marvellous things to happen.

What do I see lying ahead? I see both hopeful signs and areas where we need to invest our energies. My most hopeful signs involve the imagination. People are beginning to think outside the box even when that container is centuries old and has become venerable. It has been said that a serious problem cannot find its resolution within the paradigm in which it originated. Not long ago, women were not allowed to undertake serious studies in theology or Sacred Scripture. I rejoice in recognizing the increasing number of women among our most creative scholars. They hold the promise of insight and new orientations that are not conditioned by the patriarchal boxes that have been dominant for several millennia. Prayer, social justice, Scripture study groups and basic Christian communities also contribute to the deepening of people's spiritual lives and to building community.

Yet we do not live in an ideal world. People have always been tempted to exercise power over and to exploit one another. This human condition has had its influence on the Church, as it has on all religious organizations down through the millennia. If our Church is to succeed in preaching the Gospel of love to all humankind, its total membership will have to awaken, to become active. The lack of initiative of the vast majority of Church membership keeps our evangelizing effort constantly debilitated, depriving the world of a powerful witness. As a result, our Church continues to exercise limited influence in matters of grave global concern.

Reform begins right in our own local Church, be it our diocese or the parish or faith community to which we belong and where we are most directly involved. We are urged to help overcome the debilitating cleavage between Sunday worship and weekday life. This responsibility belongs to all of us. The liturgy is meant to strengthen and nourish the people, to accomplish their mission in proclaiming the Reign of God and building a better world. The Council insisted that all the faithful should participate "knowingly, actively, and fruitfully." Church leaders have a special responsibility to provide the conditions whereby this can happen effectively. Lay people need to insist on their rights.

I encourage people to explore how to use language, music, dance and art creatively, and how to help the clergy enhance their homilies with shared reflections based on the Scripture readings. Some may wish to help bring a better balance between contemplative and expressive worship. Various seating arrangements might improve how we experience our celebrations. I am saddened to observe what appears to be backtracking on the part of influential Church leaders in matters of subsidiarity, of overriding local authorities, of inadequate consultation, in the use of appropriate vernacular language, or lack of respect for local culture and customs.

The promotion of adult faith development, including communal discernment and sharing in decision making, in administration and management, requires special attention. This holds equally for participation in the mission of the diocese and of the parish. Our local faith communities are meant to be vibrant, inclusive, just, welcoming and joyful. Ideally, they are to be places that enliven our faith, restore our hope and deepen our commitment to our royal, prophetic and priestly calling. The formation of prayerful social action groups, such as I already perceive are multiplying around us, can further develop this commitment.

Renewal of the charismatic-prophetic aspects of Church life is required as well. It is also crucial that the Vatican Council principle of the "hierarchy of truths" – such as the centrality of Christ, the Gospel teachings, equality of all the baptized and the priority of the poor – be upheld as we plan for the future.

Our entire Church is earnestly in need of ongoing reform in view of its current loss of credibility, caused by various excesses and abuses. Critics have rightly drawn our attention to dysfunctional structures and even systemic failures. We are urged to repentance and conversion. The smug culture of secrecy must give way to a humble and honest transparency. We are admonished to relinquish our desire for power over others, to commit ourselves to the preferential option for the cause of the poor, and to move from domination and conflict towards earnest humility and devoted service to others. Society and the world are in great need of a renewed injection of Gospel values.

How can we maintain our hope and trust while facing such an enormous task? Why not begin with the words recently penned for us by Pope Benedict XVI:

> May our sorrow and our tears,
> Our sincere effort to redress past wrongs,
> And our firm purpose of amendment
> Bear an abundant harvest of grace
> For the deepening of the faith
> In our families, parishes, schools and communities,
> For the spiritual progress of our society,
> And the growth of charity, justice, joy and peace
> Within the whole human family.

There is a world consciousness becoming more manifest in local spheres. There are signs that a great awakening is indeed beginning. Foremost among the areas that require action is the reclaiming by all the baptized of their equality, dignity and capacity to serve or minister as members of the People of God. Hence there should be no evidence of privileged positions in our Church. No one is to be considered superior to another. It is our responsibility as well to discern how best we can embrace our calling as "priests, prophets and leaders," as St. Peter advised us (1 Pet. 2.9-10), in building up the world and fulfilling its purpose. To do this with a heart for justice and the cause of the poor, we can also remind ourselves of what the 1971 Synod of Bishops, following in the wake of the Council, declared: "Action on behalf of justice and participation in the transformation of the world fully appear to us as a constitutive dimension of the proclamation of the Gospel" (Article 6). There really cannot be authentic justice or meaningful preaching of the Good News if we provide no visible and tangible response to situations of manifest injustice.

We will not always agree with everyone else, but as we strive towards unity on divisive issues, we can begin with an attempt at dialogue. Pope Paul gave us a pastoral plan for such dialogue in his first encyclical, *Ecclesiam Suam*. It contains two key words: *listen* and *dialogue*. I suggest we apply this program to our own lives and activities. We truly listen when we are open to the promptings of the Holy

Spirit. We dialogue when we use the eyes and ears of our hearts as well as our bodies. That means that in the common search for truth, we always treat people with the greatest respect and attribute a positive meaning to whatever they say. In that way we can combine all our talents to promote the common good. We can only imagine how international as well as local relations would change for the better if we looked at every other person as implicated in some way in the mystery of God. If we saw that all those who strive for the good, who suffer, who mourn, who rejoice and celebrate are somehow involved in the unfolding of the divine design for the universe, what could we not begin to accomplish!

In the same way, our promotion of Christian unity can serve as a sign of dialogue for the entire Church. We all have an obligation to pray and work for the restoration of unity, and to initiate common efforts in prayer and in social action. Christ prayed that all may be one. We cannot do less than follow his example. The essential characteristics are willingness to change and openness of heart. John XXIII was reported as having said to a non-Catholic visitor that between friends, we do not focus on minor differences but on the real values we have in common. I wish that all Catholics would manifest the same compassionate hearts and open minds, and that we would be more flexible in matters of practices, amenable to different expressions of truth and more patient towards others. John XXIII's inspired leadership greatly encouraged efforts towards ecumenism, Christian unity and interfaith relationships. They received a tremendous boost from the Council when we bishops recognized that every single person of good will is in some way related to the Paschal Mystery. How attentively have we reflected on this teaching? How has it affected our attitudes?

It has been heartening for me to notice how more and more people are gathering to reflect on social issues and to undertake local initiatives for the betterment of humankind. "Think globally; act locally" has become a popular slogan. A world consciousness is becoming more manifest in local spheres. There are signs that a great awakening is indeed beginning. I am indebted to cosmologists and scholars such as Brian Swimme, Thomas Berry and Alexandra Kovats, s.s.j.p., for having awakened in me a deeper understanding of the harmony that exists throughout the entirety of creation, with the unimaginable scope of its vastness. Sunsets and sunrises, the unfolding of life in all its forms, the majesty of mountains and oceans – all have taken on a mystic quality for me. I also thank God for the indwelling spiritual inspiration that animates the contemporary "green" movement.

Vatican II encouraged us to re-examine our sacred texts: to study, reflect on and embrace their enlivening messages. From Genesis to Revelation, we are reminded that we are fashioned from the earth, meant to live in a garden of delight and to move resolutely towards the heavenly city, the New Jerusalem. Our entire planet is incorporated in this journey. Our connection to the earth is vital, as Jesus himself modelled in his teachings. At the time of Vatican II, environmental stewardship of creation was not as pronounced as it is today, nor was it in our consciousness as urgent. Since then there has been substantial progress in new earth theologies. We desperately need a dialogue between the best minds working in this domain and the policy setters and industry leaders who direct the exploration of our natural resources. The times call for great resolve. To honour and protect Mother Earth is to render homage to the Creator who also gave us Nature, which early theologians regarded as God's first book of revelation to humanity. (Early Church writers spoke of the two books of revelation: Scripture, and Nature. The "Book of Nature" could be "read" even by illiterate folk, and by its "reading" they could learn about its "author.") How do we plan to participate in this emerging synergy of science, religion and spirituality? The plight of our earth requiring our care is a sign of the times. How can we fail to acknowledge it and to respond as compassionate and committed human beings?

Finally, were I asked to designate one area where courageous leadership is needed today, I would say it was in the promotion of peace and the abolition of nuclear arms. What point is there in promoting a variety of social causes, vital as they are, if in the meantime we are putting the survival of humanity at risk? There is no sense in building an economy based on war and on obliterating the very source of our existence, or in destroying the very civilization that has been built up over centuries by the most gifted among the people who have walked this earth. Can we really think we are rational and practical when we try to solve problems by destroying people? We live in a fantasy world if we believe we have unlimited money to waste on war, but claim we cannot feed, house, clothe and educate the very people who keep us all alive.

Fifty years of lecturing and travelling have confirmed the conviction I gained after the Council: Vatican II is not for the archives! Yes, many cherished Church structures are crumbling. Yes, such disintegration is painful, and we cannot stop the movement of history. But before anyone can build on an old site, what was there in its ruins must first be cleared away. The Church appears somewhat like a ruined building in an old garden after a long and harsh winter: we observe the old trees, and see the dead and shrivelled plants. We note the crumbling stones lying around. Their work is finished. We do not resent the fact that they have passed on: it is part of the normal cycle of life and death. Vatican II bore much fruit and produced copious seed for future generations. We look to the green shoots that are emerging from the wilted beds, and to the once solid rocks that stood as a fortress, and as we take up the task of renewal, we wait in joyful hope for the promise of new life, with strength for generations to come.

Some people claim these are the worst of times. Others maintain they are the best of times. From a pastoral perspective, I remind us all that these are the *only* times. We are called to action *now*! I have met many people, young and not so young, with brave hearts and splendid ideals. I admire all the energy expended in parish endeavours and Church-sponsored or interfaith social projects.

However, to you who read these lines, I submit another consideration. There is a vast world out there, desperately in need of an infusion of Gospel values, with multitudes of people waiting to be loved into wholeness. Let us not remain focused on our internal structures and concerns. Let us not wait for others to stretch our own horizons. Today's world desperately needs our vision and our talents. Trusting in the Spirit, let each one of us reach out to our neighbour in a creative dialogue with all who care about truth and justice. Then we, too, will be beacons of light and hope for all of humankind to see.

APPENDIX I

Gaudium et Spes No. 49 – Conjugal Love
Intervention by Remi De Roo at Vatican II

The manner in which world attention is focused presently on the Church's study of family problems is a charismatic note of our times. It offers unique opportunity for a positive promotion of conjugal sanctity, to the lasting benefit of the whole People of God.

The whole Christian people must contribute to the solution of the grave problems that affect Conjugal Love. Married Life is the vocation of the vast majority of Christians. And the mind of the Faithful (*sensus fidelium*) has a special function not only in matters of doctrine or belief but in matters of Christian morals or practice as well.

The following statement reflects the thinking of a number of Canadian couples whom I consulted on the matter of Conjugal Love. These Christian couples expect the Vatican Council to recognize their proper gifts and the special characteristics of their vocation. They want encouragement and help to move with enthusiasm towards deeper conjugal life in this age of Church renewal.

To this end should we not courageously set aside too great a preoccupation with the pitfalls of married love and its ever possible abuses? Should we not insist rather on the positive vision of the riches of human love and the heights it can reach through grace? Our present schema (number 62) has succeeded only partially in this regard.

It contains some rich doctrine and values which the married people will certainly appreciate. However, by listening to the aspirations of modern Christian spouses we can realize that many elements in the text would still disappoint them deeply.

Christian spouses know that their conjugal union cannot be really understood unless a central fact of prime importance is clearly recognized. This is that marital intimacy gives rise to a unique communion by the partners of their complete lives and persons. Classical doctrine states that marriage is intended for procreation. Let us not forget, however, that procreation requires that the parents be the authors of more than physical life. They must also be a source of love for the entire family, a fountain which must never run dry. This is impossible without unfailing generosity in every aspect of their lives.

Such generosity is not acquired once and for all. It must be renewed and nourished daily as circumstances vary and needs arise. Constant expression of affection and dedication is like a sacrament of the married vocation because it both signifies and nourishes this vocation. The very quality of married love is dependent on this daily renewal.

We ignore reality if we consider merely one or the other gesture of conjugal love apart from the whole of daily family life. For the expressions of love proper to conjugal life fit into a total complex outside of which they lose their full and true meaning. Physical attraction alone fails to define married love; pleasure alone cannot describe its bounds. Christian marriage is also a vocation to seek perfection as a team and should not be set in any other context.

Married couples tell us that conjugal love is a spiritual experience of the most profound kind. It gives them their deepest insight into their own being, into what they mean to each other, into their mutual communion in unbreakable union. Through this love they grasp the mysterious purpose of their life as one, as well as the bonds that link them to God the Creator. In an almost tangible way they commune in God's love, and through their activity as spouses they see intuitively that God is the source of life and happiness.

Faith tells them that through the marriage sacrament, through their creative gestures and the liturgical life of the family, they collaborate with the Word of God drawing the whole world to His Father by His Incarnation. They provide the new members who increase the Body of Christ. They become instruments for the redemption of humanity and for the progress of the universe. God's unique creative and redemptive plan calls for the transformation of the material and spiritual world by linking humanity to God in Christ. And it is from the conjugal intimacy of the Christian home that Christ today first finds this humanity He has come to redeem.

The creative function of conjugal love spreads its influence beyond the home as well. In union with other couples, spouses who fully serve their family build the total temporal community where people may achieve their proper destiny. The family founded on true conjugal love is a witness to society and a leaven through which joy and happiness are spread.

These are but some of the reasons why spouses must never abstain from constant development of authentic conjugal love and its practice. Arbitrary norms drawn from external considerations have little value in this domain.

In view of the above we see how our pastoral concern for the perfection of conjugal love serves not only the Church but also the whole of human society. Not for a moment would we think of minimizing the need for precise legislation by the Church on this gravest of matters. But this vital framework of laws must not inhibit the full development of Christian married love in all its dimensions. And we must promote and emphasize positively the unique redemptive values of Christian conjugal love.

We should not hesitate to recognize also the medicinal value of marital intimacy. Husband and wife find it is often indispensable when spirits are dejected, when a partner labors under some extreme difficulty, when home life has lost the serenity so necessary for the children's welfare. For when we speak of conjugal union, not only the parents are involved but the children as well. Christian conjugal love overflows to the children and all those associated with the home. Pastoral experience knows this for a fact.

This Council will promote the redemption of all humanity by speaking frankly of the positive values of conjugal love. Never has the world so needed to recognize the divine plan whereby humans are associated with divine creative love and thus discover their true dignity: "God created man in his image. In the Image of God he created him. Male and female he created them. Then God blessed them and said to them, 'Be fruitful and multiply; fill the earth and subdue it'" (Genesis 1, 27-28). Revised in the light of the above remarks, this statement on Conjugal Love would be welcomed with enthusiasm and gratitude by the Christian couples of the world. The growing number of family organizations and the rising currents of conjugal spirituality which we joyfully hail today could find the inspiration and the guidance they ardently desire in this doctrine. Would not such teaching lead to a greater appreciation of authentic conjugal love in the life and thought of the entire Church?

Appendix II

Proclamation of the Synod for the Diocese of Victoria

31 October 1986
Vigil of the Feast of All Saints

Dear brothers and sisters in Christ: RE: DIOCESAN SYNOD

By this pastoral letter I wish to announce the convocation of a Diocesan Synod for all the Catholic faithful on Vancouver Island.

The Second Vatican Council was in session when my appointment as Bishop of Victoria was announced twenty-four years ago on October 31st, 1962. And so I felt that the vigil of All Saints day was an appropriate occasion to launch our Synod. In effect, the Council reminded us that we are all saints through faith and baptism, equal in dignity and in capacity to serve through a variety of ministries. Ours is the mission to proclaim the coming of God's Realm throughout the universe.

Our mission to Church and Society is often described in four Greek words: KERYGMA, LITURGIA, KOINONIA, DIAKONIA. These can be translated approximately as PROCLAMATION, WORSHIP, COMMUNION, SERVICE.

We will keep these four aspects in mind as we consider how effectively the Second Vatican Council has been lived on Vancouver Island and what further growth the Holy Spirit is calling us to achieve for the Glory of God.

The synodal process will be given adequate time to achieve its objectives and thus may well span two or three years. The important thing is to ensure the greatest possible degree of fruitful participation.

Since we are dealing with matters of the Spirit and the promotion of God's Reign, prayer is of the essence. I invite all the faithful of our Diocese to pray regularly for the success of this undertaking.

The Synod deliberations will follow a process of spiritual discernment. All participants will be invited to familiarize themselves with this prayerful method of discussing issues and reaching conclusions by consensus. We will seek to avoid superficial managerial decision making, political confrontation or any other approach based on power and not on the spirit of service to the Reign of God. I have asked members of the Prayer Companion movement to be available where required to initiate people into this process of spiritual discernment.

As soon as convenient, I will personally visit every parish to explain the nature and purpose of the Synod as well as to invite everyone to participate. On that occasion, I hope to meet representatives from every parish organization. Volunteers will be required to help formulate proposals, stimulate discussion and promote development in all key areas of Catholic life. By way of example, one could mention family life concerns, ecumenism, liturgy, administration, outreach and hospitality, evangelisation and other areas of concern.

Therefore, I declare the following:

In the Name of the Father, and of the Son and of the Holy Spirit.

A diocesan synod is hereby convened for all the faithful of the diocese of Victoria on Vancouver Island and adjacent diocesan territory. The purpose of the Synod will be as follows:

– To further proclaim the good news of the Realm of God by professing our faith in Christ Jesus Our Lord.

– To pray for the continued guidance of the Holy Spirit as we seek to fulfill the will of our Heavenly Father.

– To assess the effect on our lives of the Second Vatican Council and its application to Vancouver Island.

- To recognize the strengths and weaknesses affecting our progress as pilgrims in faith.

- To render thanks to God for the blessings imparted through the Council.

- To discern the continuing call of the Holy Spirit towards new growth in a variety of ministries and services to society.

- To establish such policies, guidelines and legislation as deemed useful for greater effectiveness, concord and unity in promoting the mission of the Church.

- To seek reconciliation of all who have been alienated for whatever cause.

- To develop and strengthen the bonds which link Roman Catholics to people of other faiths.

- To dedicate ourselves to work with all people of good will in transforming society and in promoting a civilization of love based on justice and peace.

Sincerely in Christ,
Remi J. De Roo, Bishop of Victoria

INDEX

Numbered references in italics are to photographs in the 16-page photo section.

Numbered references in italics are to photographs in the 16-page photo section.

Numbered references in italics are to photographs in the 16-page photo section.

Numbered references in italics are to photographs in the 16-page photo section.

S

Sahale Stick *7B*
Schuta, Roger *13A*
Semina Verbi 68
Sensus fidelium 111, 165
Sexton, Harold 82, 89, *7A*
Shepherd, Ronald *4B*
Sisters of St. Ann 80, 130, 148
Sisters of St. Joseph of Carondelet,
    Los Angeles 148
Sisters of the Immaculate Heart of
    Mary 8, 130, 131
Sisters of the Love of Jesus 125
Smith, Henry *10A*
Sobrino, Jon 101
Social Affairs Commission 96, 99, 100,
    103
Social justice 64, 65, 72, 86, 90, 94, 95,
    102, 158
    office of 90
Social solidarity 103, 104
    Working Committee for 102
Society of the Divine Word 144
St. Boniface Cathedral 79
St. Boniface College 21, 26, 27
St. Boniface Hospital 33
St. Boniface (Winnipeg) 31, 38, 79
St. Gerard School 23
St. Joan's Alliance 46
St. Mary's Priory, Colwood 125
St. Michael's Church, Calgary 148
St. Patrick's, Seattle 147
Saint Paul University, Ottawa 147
St. Peter's Basilica 16, 30, 36, 38, 42,
    45, 52
St. Vincent de Paul 90
Stangl, Joanne *2B*
Stangl, Joseph C. *2B*
Stangl, Judith *2B*
Stangl, Katherine *2B*
Subsidiarity 53, 75, 159
Suenens, Leo Josef 46, 57
Swan Lake, Manitoba 21, 29, 68, 83, *1A*
Swimme, Brian 161
Synod

early use 107
process 109ff.
proclamation of 110
promulgation of 118
roots of, in Victoria 108
Synod of Bishops 42, 67, 100, 132, 133,
    160

T

Thomas, Coreen 97
Tolomeo, Diane *16B*

U

Underwood, Ed *6A*
United Nations 66, 98, 102
United Peasants' Committee 102
University of Louvain 101, 146
University of Victoria
    archives 94
    Centre for Studies in Religion
    and Society 147
    chaplaincy 89–90
    students 91

V

Van de Voorde, Marie Therese 138
Vanier, Jean 90, 149
Veni Sancte Spiritus 116
Vernacular 74, 93, 159
Viri probati 75, 131, 134

W

Ward, Barbara 46
Whelan, Eugene 104
Winandy, Jacques 40
Women
    at Council 45–47
    conference in Washington, D.C.
    131–133
    role in the Church 56, 69, 71, 89,
    94, 131
    Women's Committee 91, 98

Numbered references in italics are to photographs in the 16-page photo section.